The Professional Development Seminar

Junior and Senior Course

Second Edition

Nichols College Professional
Development Staff and Faculty

Kendall Hunt
publishing company

Cover image © Nichols College

Kendall Hunt
publishing company

www.kendallhunt.com
Send all inquiries to:
4050 Westmark Drive
Dubuque, IA 52004-1840

Copyright © 2010 by Nichols College Professional Development Faculty and Staff

ISBN 978-0-7575-7416-0

Kendall Hunt Publishing Company has the exclusive rights to reproduce this work,
to prepare derivative works from this work, to publicly distribute this work,
to publicly perform this work and to publicly display this work.

All rights reserved. No part of this publication may be reproduced,
stored in a retrieval system, or transmitted, in any form or by any
means, electronic, mechanical, photocopying, recording, or otherwise,
without the prior written permission of the copyright owner.

Printed in the United States of America
10 9 8 7 6 5 4 3

Thank you to the PDS Staff and Faculty who contributed to this workbook.

TABLE OF CONTENTS

NOTES

JUNIOR AND SENIOR COURSES

~~~

Professional Development Seminar (PDS)

The Junior and Senior courses in this book are designed to be the third and fourth components in a series of four courses. However, each can be used as individual courses designed to meet the career and professional developmental needs of college juniors and/or seniors.

NOTES

OUTLINE OF PDS COURSES

	FIRST-YEAR "Transition & Adjustment"	SOPHOMORE "Exploration"	JUNIOR "Refinement"	SENIOR "Implementation"
Wk #	Fall Semester	Spring Semester	Spring Semester	Fall Semester
1	College Transition; Goal Setting	Course Preview; Intro. to Portfolios	Course Preview; Portfolios	Course Preview; Portfolios; Senior Group Projects
2	Time Management	Portfolio: Purpose, Content, Format, Materials	Resumes – Electronic & Paper; Cover Letters, Professional Letters	Recruiting Options - On/Off-Campus, Individual Plan
3	Academic Success	Self Exploration; Role of Education	Professional Presentation; Communication Skills	Using the Portfolio in an Interview
4	Library Skills	Academic & Career Planning; Academic Fair	Intro. to Interviewing, Questions Asked/To Ask	Money/Budgeting
5	Relationships	Resumes-Content	Interviewing In-depth, How to Work a Career Fair	Senior Choice Programs**
6	Health & Wellness	Resumes-Format	Mock Interviews	Senior Choice Programs**
7	Campus Awareness	Sophomore Choice Programs*	Mock Interviews	Senior Choice Programs**
8	Academic Advising/ Course Registration	Professional Letter Writing; Email Etiquette	Mock Interviews	MBTI & Assessments
9	Professionalism; Portfolios	Portfolio Introductory Statement; Portfolio Review Session	Mock Interviews	Business Etiquette; Ethics; Networking
10	Career Development	How to Make a Prof. Presentation with the Portfolio; Portfolio Review Session	Portfolio Review Session	Presentations: Senior Group Projects
11	Presentations	Presentations with Portfolio	Multiculturalism, Options after Graduation, Generations	Presentations: Senior Group Projects
12	Presentations; Course Evaluation	Presentations with Portfolio; Course Evaluation; Portfolio Due	Presentations about Informational Interviews; Course Evaluation; Portfolios Due	Affective/Transition Topics; First Year on the Job; Course Evaluation; Portfolios Due

* Sophomore Choice Programs: No regular class meeting for week #7 – sophomores must attend at least 1 of 3 programs/events offered: Career Fair, Interviewing Skills, and Internship Opportunities.

** Senior Choice Programs: No regular class meeting for the month of October - seniors must attend 4 of about 25 programs offered. Most programs are led by corporate recruiters and/or alumni. Topics include: Negotiating Salary & Benefits, First Year on the Job, Resumes/Cover Letters In-depth, Mock Interview with a Recruiter, Women in Business, Using the Internet for a Job Search, Networking, Etiquette Dinner, Experience-Sharing with a First-Year PDS Class, Career Options for Liberal Arts Majors, Renting an Apartment/Buying a Car, Advanced Interviewing Skills, Staying Fit for Life, Post-graduation Options, Career Options in Retail Management, Graduate School Information, Law School Information.

STUDENT & EMPLOYER TESTIMONIALS

"The skills learned through the mock interviews are priceless. Being taught how to be utilizing your portfolio as a marketing tool is also a timeless skill to have."   ~ Student

"The skills learned there (in the PDS program) are not ubiquitous amongst the other graduates in New England. Time and time again I am working with members of the senior class at a New England institution who have no concept of how to act in an interview scenario. Too many times have I seen spelling errors and grammatical errors on resumes and students not knowing how to turn a leadership position on campus into marketable, valuable experience."

~Alumni

"In my opinion, the portfolios allow students to compile all of their best work which can then be shown to potential employers. I will continue to update my portfolio as a working professional, and I'll enjoy looking through the contents of my portfolio for many years to come. I am proud of what I accomplished at Nichols College, and I think the portfolios are a great assignment in the PDS program even though they are very time consuming. Overall, I found the PDS program to be beneficial. Each semester I learned something new that has helped me to better prepare for my future."   ~Student

"I think that the mock interviews, and the teachings of what we are supposed to say, and how to act was very professional and helpful."   ~Student

The PDS program at Nichols College is second to none in preparing students to enter the workforce. The portfolio that students create over their 4 years in school sets them apart from other candidates when they interview as it gives them an opportunity to visually show all that they have accomplished and the strengths that they will bring to a job.   ~Recruiter

"The PDS program gave me confidence in interviewing."   ~Student

"The PDS program was a huge help for me!!! Being able to do so many practice interviews at Nichols helped me ace the real thing when it counted! I would recommend that all students take advantage of the PDS program because it really does help with developing the skills you are going to use on an everyday basis in the real world. "   ~Student

"The PDS program was a great asset to NC, we learned a lot. I have a lot of friends that graduated in 2005 and before then and none of them had a comparable program available at their colleges."

~Student

"I work with and recruit students throughout different colleges in Central Mass. And I have found that Nichols students consistently stand out among the rest. I think this is in large part due to Nichols' own PDS program!"
                                                                                                ~Recruiter

"The Connecticut State Police is always impressed with the quality of Nichols Students!"
                                                                                    ~ Recruiter

"I feel that the interviewing skills came in handy with the job I currently have. I am a Background Investigator with an independent company. I do investigations everyday where I have to interview people. I feel that the interview process in the PDS classes also prepared me for interviews in applying for jobs. I knew how to handle myself, how to dress, and how to act. I feel that Nichols trained us very well in the interviewing process."   ~Alumni

"The portfolio is a priceless tool! Whether or not you use it in an actual interview depends; but it definitely makes the entire interview process easier and less stressful. My portfolio has been my best study guide during all my interviews! It helped me prepare for basic interview questions such as tell us about yourself?, what skills do you have?, what qualities do you possess?, what has your coursework prepared you for? etc..."   ~Student

"Nichols College students really stand apart from students at other colleges I recruit at. Through the PDS program and the portfolio process, I notice that students from Nichols have a more clear perception of themselves and their strengths and weaknesses. They have been coached about how to speak and communicate in interviews, and it shows. The PDS program gets them started working on those skills early enough that they are able to interview well, even after their sophomore year. Nichols students also are able to articulate their skills, experience, and enthusiasm better. I thoroughly enjoy interviewing students from Nichols College and look forward to continuing to build strong relationships with the college and its students in the future."
                                                                                    ~Recruiter

"If you want to make something of yourself in life then you will take PDS seriously, because everything PDS covers is relevant and useful in the real world!"
                                                                                    ~Student

"I think PDS is more than a class... It's an essential to know the proper techniques of interviewing, resume writing, and business etiquette. PDS really teaches you how to be professional during an interview."   ~Student

Over the past two years, we have hired high quality Nichols students for the Executive Intern and Executive Team Leader position who are now very successful at Target. Nichols does an amazing job of preparing their students to be professional and enter the workforce.
                                                                                    ~ Recruiter

NOTES

JUNIOR AND SENIOR COURSES

Portfolio Information

NOTES

INTRODUCTION TO THE PORTFOLIO

What is a Portfolio?
A portfolio is a collection of materials representing you as an individual and your experiences in college. It is not limited in contents and allows flexibility in regards to its contents.

What does a Portfolio contain?
The possible contents in a portfolio are numerous; however, the following provides some ideas:

- Professional cover with name
- Table of contents
- Introductory statement
- Resume
- Work samples
- Summaries of independent readings
- Reviews of independent readings
- Reviews of internships, jobs, training programs, volunteer work, etc…
- Travel study
- Organization memberships
- Awards
- Recommendation letters
- Pictures/photographs
- Significant school projects
- Writing samples
- Computer disks with projects (i.e.; power point)
- High score exams
- Transcripts
- Lesson plans, evaluations, materials and teaching philosophies from student teaching experiences.
- Future goals
- Reflective statements about portfolio, professional experiences, internships, etc…
- Volunteer/Community Service Experience
- Letters of reference

Who sees my Portfolio?
You may share your portfolio with potential employers, interviewers for graduate school, and professors.

Why use a Portfolio?
- It shows initiative
- It shows organization and preparedness
- It shows verification
- It is tangible evidence that cannot be found on a resume

PORTFOLIO CONTENTS

Items Needed:

1) 3-ring binder with clear plastic cover
2) Plastic sheet protectors (30-100)
3) Plastic sheet protectors with attached tabs for title pages (8-12)
4) Professional-looking stationary for cover and title pages (or print graphic or border on plain paper)

Portfolio Contents (the portfolio must include the following):

1) Cover with name
2) Table of Contents
3) Introductory Statement
4) Resume
5) Required Categories (see below)
6) Optional Categories (see below)
7) Letters of Reference

Required Categories (at least two items per category in the sophomore year with the addition of one or more new items added in each of the junior and senior years):

1) Career and Professional Planning/Growth – career goals, outstanding work in the major, internship experience, professional membership, job shadow experience/informational interview, etc.
2) Teamwork/Leadership Skills – clubs/activities, athletics, team projects, leadership roles, etc.
3) Communication Skills – examples of oral and/or written work.
4) Analytical/Problem Solving/Critical Thinking Skills – research projects, examples of an ability to develop, analyze and interpret information, etc.
5) Technology Related Skills – PowerPoint demonstrations, computer programming/application, demonstration of video/audio skills, etc.

Optional Categories (must include at least one each year):

1) Arts/Culture – participation/experience in music, theatre, art; personal experience in other cultures, study of other cultures, etc.
2) Volunteer Experience/ Community Service – volunteer experience, participation (formal and/or informal) in community activities and organizations
3) Other - an experience in life that has special meaning or has allowed for significant learning. ex.: extensive travel, study abroad, participation in a unique group, participation in an extraordinary event, a special hobby, etc.

Professional Presentation of Items:

1) All items must be presented professionally:

- typed (not handwritten) captions, tabs, headings, etc.
- organization – tabs, title pages, an order that allows quick access
- attach/glue items carefully , no tape showing, etc.
- use plastic sheet covers to protect work
- use a presentation theme that carries through the portfolio – same font and size for all headings, same paper/style for title pages, etc.
- use visuals – pictures, graphs, brochures, flyers, etc.
- use color ink and color pictures whenever possible

2) All items in the categories listed above should have an explanation/description:

- what the item is
- when it was completed
- why it is included – its significance, what was learned from this project or event, skills developed or enhanced, etc.

3) Support knowledge or skill with pictures, examples of work, certificates, etc.

Other Considerations:

The portfolio should demonstrate knowledge/experience in the major and this theme should be carried throughout the portfolio. The skills/learning in the major should be demonstrated consistently and repeatedly. For example, projects, papers and presentations in major classes should be included. Teamwork/Leadership skills may also define the skills gained/needed for a particular major. The preparation undertaken for the major should be demonstrated in the Career and Professional Planning/Growth category. The reader of the portfolio should have a clear understanding of the major and the steps taken to date to prepare for a career in this area.

The focus for the development of the portfolio is for use in career preparation. The portfolio should be prepared with the intended reader as a corporate recruiter or hiring manager for an internship and/or full-time position upon graduation. If graduate school is the next step, then preparation of the portfolio should be focused on use with a graduate admissions officer, and perhaps later for use in seeking employment.

Evaluation of the Portfolio:

Portfolio Sections: evaluated for content quality and quantity	
Career and Professional Planning Growth	13%
Teamwork/Leadership Skills	13%
Communication Skills	13%
Analytical/Problem Solving/Critical Thinking Skills	13%
Technology Related Skills	13%
Optional Category	13%
Portfolio Presentation- Organization, Professional Presentation, Neatness	12%
Additional Items- Cover, Table of Contents, Intro. Statement, Resume, Reference	10%
Total	100%

NOTES

Professional Development Seminar Program

PORTFOLIO CONTENTS WORKSHEET

	SOPHOMORE (minimum 2 items)	JUNIOR (minimum 3 items)	SENIOR (minimum 4 items)
REQUIRED CATEGORIES (% of final portfolio grade)			
Career and Professional Planning/Growth (13%)			
Teamwork/Leadership Skills (13%)			
Communication Skills (13%)			
Analytical/Problem Solving/Critical Thinking (13%)			
Technology Related Skills (13%)			
ADDITIONAL CATEGORIES (13%) include minimum number of items across 3 categories			
Arts/Culture			
Volunteer Experience/ Community Service			
Other – see description			
PORTFOLIO PRESENTATION – Organization, Professional Presentation, Neatness (12%)			
ADDITIONAL REQUIRED ITEMS – (10%)			

* COVER WITH NAME   * TABLE OF CONTENTS   * INTRODUCTORY STATEMENT

* RESUME   * LETTER(S) OF REFERENCE

13

PORTFOLIO DESCRIPTIONS WORKSHEET

The purpose of this exercise is to get you to think critically about the items you choose to include in your portfolio. It is necessary for you to write a description of each item placed it in the portfolio. This form is designed to facilitate that process. Once portfolio items are selected, you should answer a series of questions about that item to explain its significance. The answers to these questions will allow you to create a thorough description for each of the items you include.

WORKSHEET:

Section of the Portfolio: _____

Item 1

What is it?

When did you do it?

Why did you choose to include it in your portfolio?

What did you learn from doing this assignment/test/project/etc.?

What skills or knowledge related to career and professional planning and growth were used to complete this item?

EXAMPLE:

Section in the Portfolio: TEAMWORK/LEADERSHIP SKILLS

<u>Item 1</u>

What is it? Presented here is the final group presentation of our virtual business "Four Paws Pet Care".

When did you do it? The project and presentation were completed in the fall of 2007 for my Business and Society class, which was taken in my freshman year.

Why did you choose to include it in your portfolio? This is the result of a semester long project I did with four other students. I am proud of this group project because we worked well together to accomplish our goal and received high marks for our efforts.

What did you learn from doing this assignment/test/project/etc.? We learned how to do market research, determine an operational budget, recruit and retain customers, and put together a plan to expand the business as profits increased.

What skills or knowledge related to teamwork/leadership were used to complete this item? Each group member brought a different set of skills, knowledge, and motivation to this project. It was a challenge at first to work with so many different people, but we found a way to get past those differences and develop a project we could all contribute to and find worthwhile. We took turns serving as group leader for various sections of the project, something that allowed each of us a chance to learn and develop effective leadership skills.

PORTFOLIO EVALUATION FORM

Student Name: _____   Semester: ___ Fall 20___

PDS Level: ___Sophomore ___Junior ___Senior   ___ Spring 20___

		Points Rec'd	% Value	Category Totals
Required Elements:				
Cover with Name		____	2%	
name	1%			
professional, neat	1%			
Table of Contents		____	2%	
neat, organized	1%			
complete	1%			
Introductory Statement		____	2%	
professional, clear	1%			
up to date	1%			
Resume		____	2%	
professional, neat	1%			
up to date	1%			
Letter(s) of Reference			2%	
more than one	1%			
dated within year	1%	____		

Subtotal:			10%	_____

Required Categories:				
Career/Prof. Planning .... ____			13%	
descriptions	3%	____		
quantity/variety	5%	____		
quality/skills	5%	____		
Teamwork/Leadership .... ____			13%	
descriptions	3%	____		
quantity/variety	5%	____		
quality/skills	5%	____		
Communication Skills .... ____			13%	
descriptions	3%	____		
quantity/variety	5%	____		
quality/skills	5%	____		
Analytical/Prob. Solving .... ____			13%	
descriptions	3%	____		
quantity/variety	5%	____		
quality/skills	5%	____		
Technology .... ____			13%	
descriptions	3%	____		
quantity/variety	5%	____		
quality/skills	5%	____		

Subtotal:			65%	_____

Optional Category: .... ____   13%
    Arts/Culture
        descriptions   3%   ____
        quantity/variety 5%   ____
        quality/skills   5%   ____
--OR--
    Volunteer, Community Service
        descriptions   3%   ____
        quantity/variety 5%   ____
        quality/skills   5%   ____
--OR--
    Other
        descriptions   3%   ____
        quantity/variety 5%   ____
        quality/skills   5%   ____

	Subtotal:	13%	_____

Portfolio Presentation: .... ____   12%
    organization   4%   ____
    professional   4%   ____
    neat   4%   ____

	Subtotal:	12%	_____

	TOTAL:	**100%**	_____
	PORTFOLIO GRADE:		_____

Comments:

JUNIOR COURSE

Week #1: Welcome and Introductions, Course Preview, Portfolio Contents

NOTES

COURSE SYLLABUS

Faculty/Instructor: Office Hours:
Telephone: Office Location:
E-mail:

Course Purpose: "Building Career Skills and the Individual Portfolio"

Course Objective:
To provide the college junior with experiential education in the interview process while providing the opportunity to enhance the portfolio and resume within ethical and professional standards. To provide educational continuity in career exploration and portfolio development from the sophomore to senior level courses.

Course Description:
The Junior course is designed to set a framework for career decision making, refining interview skills, and developing an individual presentation through the portfolio. The heart of the course is the expanded development of the student portfolio, a collection of each student's work, goals, experiences, accomplishments and achievements. Students will expand the portfolio with an emphasis on their individual achievement and success. Another focus of the course is gaining interview experience through 4 weeks of mock interviews both as an interviewer and interviewee. Additionally, the class includes other relevant career topics as professionalism, communication skills, and post-graduation options.

Term of Course: Class will meet once a week for twelve weeks.

Course Outline:
Date:

Week #1:	**Welcome and Introductions, Course Preview** **Portfolio Contents for Junior Year** Begin portfolio additions/revisions
Week #2:	**Resumes (paper and electronic), Cover Letters, Employment Letters** *Assignment due week #3:* Updated resume
Week #3:	**Professional Presentation/Communication Skills** *Assignment:* Continue with portfolio additions/revisions
Week #4:	**Introduction to Interviewing** *Assignments due week #5:* Finalize resume, print on resume paper, and bring to next class to give to interview partner. Participate in Alumni Career Day; date/time TBA

Week #5:   **Interviewing In-depth**
              Assignment due on mock interview date:
              Prepare for mock interview- practice questions/responses
              Items to be submitted at mock interview (typed):
                  o   Interviewer:
                       Form: Interviewer Questions for Interviewee
                  o   Interviewee:
                       Form: Company/Position Information Form (research on
                       company, company summary *in your own words*)
                       Form: Interviewee Questions for Interviewer
                       Resume on resume paper

Week #6:   **Mock Interviews**

Week #7:   **Mock Interviews**

Week #8:   **Mock Interviews**
              Assignment due week #9:
              Complete the DISCOVER surveys online (interest, abilities, values) and
              print 2 copies of the summary page – one for you and one for the
              professor/instructor to be turned in at class #9.

Week #9:   **Mock Interviews**
              Assignment due week #10:
              Finalize draft of portfolio.

Week #10:   **Draft Portfolio Review Session with Portfolio Coordinator**
              Small group meetings with Portfolio Coordinator in lieu of class. Bring your
              draft portfolio with you to the meeting. Date/time TBA.
              Assignment due week #11:
              Complete portfolio.

Week #11:   **Post- Graduation Options/Graduate School/Multiculturism**
              PORTFOLIO DUE AT CLASS
              Assignment due week #12:
              Research options and complete 2 forms.

Week #12:   **Presentations about Information Interview/Course Evaluation**

(Dates)	Graded portfolios available from Faculty/Instructor

Grading: Final Grades will be composed of the following elements:

Updated resume	10%
Participate in mock interview	40%
(effort, preparation & quality)	
Portfolio	30%
DISCOVER	10%
Class Participation (including attendance at	10%
Alumni Career Day and Career Fair)	
	100%

PROFESSIONAL MEMBERSHIP ORGANIZATIONS

<u>Assignment due Week 2</u>:

Research professional organizations in the field you want to work in (ex.: American Marketing Association, New England Human Resources Association, etc.).

Select 2 professional organizations.

Write a 2 page paper about the 2 professional organizations.

Contents: items to consider including in the paper:

- Introduction

- Organization: The full name of the organization, where it is located/operates, a brief history, its purpose/mission, its effectiveness.

- Members: Why people join, the requirements to become a member, the type of person/professional who joins, the number of members, what benefits members receive, the cost/terms of membership.

- Organizational activities: The type of activities the organization offers, conferences/workshops provided, the advocacy the organization is involved with, services available to members.

- Your Involvement: Why would/do you want to join these organizations? What will your level of involvement be? What do you expect to get out of membership in this organization? What is it about this organization that interests you?

- Conclusion

Format: 12 font, double space, 1inch margins, 2 pages.

A good source to find organizations related to your area of study is:

   http://www.weddles.com/associations

INFORMATIONAL INTERVIEW ASSIGNMENT

What is an Informational Interview?
An informational interview is an interview designed to give you, the student interviewer, information and insight into a particular position, company, or career path. While contacts may be developed by participating in this process, the focus is the information gathered. *You should not ask for a job in this process.* However, if the opportunity to apply for a position is offered by the person being interviewed, it may be accepted.

Who Should I Interview?
Any knowledgeable person in the field of your interest would be helpful. Obviously, the higher the person is in the company, the more information you will gather on a broader scale. If your interest is in a specific position, then locate someone in that particular position. You may not interview a relative.

How Do I Locate Someone to Interview?
To find someone, consider all of the people you know who may have contacts with someone in the field. If you are not able to locate someone on your own, your faculty member or the staff in the Alumni Office or Office of Career Services will be glad to help you brainstorm some options.

How will I contact/interview this person?
For this assignment, you will need to meet with someone *in person* for the interview, but you may contact him/her initially by email or telephone to set up the interview.

When Should I Interview Someone?
Call or email the person you wish to interview several weeks before the assignment is due. They will be more willing to be helpful to you if they have some flexibility about scheduling a time to meet. The informational interview must be completed in the current semester (prior informational interviews will not count).

What Should I Say to Them on the Telephone or in an Email?
Introduce yourself and tell them you would like to conduct an informational interview with them because... (they are well known in the field, they come highly recommended as someone who is influential the field, or they were recommended by _____). Always acknowledge that you know that they are very busy and that you are willing to work around their availability.

What Do I Bring With Me to the Informational Interview?
Bring a list of your questions (be sure to do a thorough research of the company before writing them), paper, a pen, your smile and a positive attitude! Learn the company dress code prior to your visit and dress appropriately.

After the Informational Interview
Be sure to get the person's business card so you may send them a thank you note. This is a very important step – don't forget!

Assignment
1) Write a 2 page paper on your reflections of the Informational Interview. Include the questions you asked. Attach the person's business card to your paper as verification of meeting him/her.
2) Prepare a 5 minute presentation about your Informational Interview. Be sure to include the name and title of who you interviewed a summary of your interview, and what you learned. Presentations will take place in class in week #12.

JUNIOR YEAR INFORMATION SHEET

Name: Home Phone: Major:

Nichols Email: Personal Email:

1. Career Goals: (Be as specific as possible at this point – field/industry, position(s), companies, etc.)

2. How do you intend to find a job before graduation?

3. Have you completed an internship? If so, where, and what was your title? Do you plan to complete one (or another) before graduation?

4. List topics that you are interested in learning about in Junior PDS and/or things you would like to cover this semester:

5. List topics or aspects about Junior PDS that you are not particularly interested in:

6. What is your goal for Junior PDS?

7. Who was your Second Year (sophomore) PDS instructor?

NOTES

26

JUNIOR COURSE

Week # 2: Resumes, Cover Letters, Employment Letters

NOTES

RESUME WRITING

A resume is a digest of your educational and occupational activities. The purpose of your resume is to advertise yourself, and to get an interview. To create a winning resume, you need to portray your strongest and most relevant achievements, be concise, factual, and project a good image; all on a single page.

I.   Organization
       1. Develop a list of your work experience, education, achievements, skills and abilities.
       2. Edit the list to capture the most important/relevant topics.

II. Types of Resumes
       1. Paper Resumes
           A. Chronological – Lists internships and employment with the most recent job first; includes job titles and company names. This is the best type of resume for most college students.
           B. Functional – Lists experience by function/type of work, targeting skill groups, focusing on transferable skills. This is the best type for job seekers switching careers and for those returning to the job market after many years away.
           C. Combination – combines the previous two.
       2. Electronic Resumes
           A. With technology being the number one tool for employers and job seekers, you will need an electronic resume for two main reasons. First, most medium to large sized organizations require job seekers to paste their resume on their website. The best way to do this without sending the employer a page of garbled text is to create an electronic, or text resume. Second, employers often scan resumes into computer databases for storing, filtering, and easy retrieval using "key words." Use resources in the Office of Career Services to research how to correctly write an electronic resume.

III. Resume Content
       1. <u>Identification</u>
           A. Name, address, telephone number, email at the top of the page. Your name should be in 18-24 font, the rest of the resume in 11-12.
           B. If you live on campus or away from your permanent address, include both your current and permanent contact information.
       2. <u>Objective</u>
           A. Include a brief, descriptive objective geared to the type of industry and/or position you seek to give your resume a clear focus.
       3. <u>Profile</u> (or Professional Summary)
           A. Optional category, challenging to write effectively.
           B. Write in detail (one line) about each of 3-5 personal attributes.
       4. <u>Education</u>
           A. Most recent college experience first; always include graduation date.
           B. Do not include high school information.

5. <u>Related Courses</u> (or Related Coursework)
   A. Optional category – include only if space permits, work experience
      and extra-curricular activities are more important. If you choose to
      include this section, list only upper-level courses and those that reflect
      relevant skills: Effective Speaking, Professional Writing, etc.
6. <u>Awards and Activities</u> (or Extra-Curricular Activities and Awards)
   A. Include the word Awards in the title only if you have awards (Dean's
      List is considered to be an award).
   B. List honors/awards, clubs, on- and off-campus activities, sports, etc.
   C. Add specific year(s) of participation.
   D. Include leadership roles- can indent next line and list title with year(s).
7. <u>Internship(s)</u>
   A. Name and location of company.
   B. Dates of internship.
   C. Position title.
   D. List responsibilities in 3-5 sentences using paragraph form or with
      bullets. Always start each sentence with an action word.
8. <u>Work Experience</u> (or Employment or Professional Experience or Related
   Experience)
   A. Use same format as outlined in steps A. – D. above under Internships.
   B. List current/most recent job first, then next most recent, etc.
   C. Include more detail with jobs that relate to the type of position you
      seek, and minimize the least relevant jobs.
   D. Include your accomplishments in addition to your duties.
   E. Quantify – "Increased sales by 10% in the second quarter as member
      of the sales team"; "Coordinated activities for 42 children in a busy
      after school program"; "Developed a new computerized process for accounts
      payable which resulted in a savings of 30 work hours per week for the
      department"
9. <u>Skills</u> (or Additional Skills or Professional Skills)
   A. Optional – include only if relevant.
   B. Certifications
   C. Languages – i.e. Fluent in French, speak Spanish conversationally,
      ability to use Sign Language.
   D. Other experiences that are unique to you – extensive travel to other
      countries, lived in another country, etc.
10. <u>Volunteer Experience</u> (or Community Service)
    A. Optional category.
    B. Positions for which you are not paid.
    C. Include title (i.e. Coach or Volunteer), organization's name and
       location, year(s).
11. <u>Computer Skills</u> (or Technological Skills)
    A. List most important/unique skills first.
    B. Include skills acquired at jobs.
12. <u>References</u>
    A. Do not list your references on your resume. You may list a heading
       followed by, "Available Upon Request" or "Furnished Upon Request"
       or, "References Available Upon Request" can be centered at the
       bottom of the page.
    B. Create a separate page using the same heading as your resume
       entitled, "References." Provide this to employers upon request.

IV.   Key Resume Tips:

1. Check spelling and grammar! Have someone else also check.
2. Do not use the pronoun "I"
3. Use action words to start each sentence in the Internship and Employment sections.
4. Add a personal touch – rather than using a cookie cutter resume.
5. Create a resume that is eye-catching and easy to read – professional, clear font with bold and italics used sparingly and consistently.
6. The most important items need to be easy to find (in 10 seconds or less) – your name, contact information, objective, college name, major, graduation date, awards and activities, and company name/job title for employment.
7. No less than ½" margins on all sides
8. Use plain white, ivory or light gray resume paper.
9. Use size 11-12 font, name in 18-24.
10. The same type of font is best throughout the resume, but your name could be a different font. If using 2 fonts, be sure they are complementary.
11. Do not fold your resume before faxing or scanning; do not staple.
12. Do not include personal data – i.e. age, marital status, height, hobbies, etc.
13. The result should be a clean, attractive, concise, and accurate record which describes you and your most relevant skills and accomplishments.

ACTION WORDS – RESUME WRITING

Accelerated	Combined	Gathered	Overhauled	Reorganized
Accessed	Converted	Generated	Oversaw	Served
Achieved	Coordinated	Guided	Participated	Set up
Acquired	Corrected	Halved	Performed	Settled
Activated	Counseled	Handled	Persuaded	Shaped
Adapted	Created	Headed	Pinpointed	Showed
Addressed	Cultivated	Helped	Pioneered	Simplified
Administered	Decreased	Hired	Planned	Sold
Advanced	Defined	Identified	Prepared	Solved
Advised	Delegated	Implemented	Presented	Specified
Allocated	Delivered	Improved	Prevented	Sponsored
Analyzed	Demonstrated	Increased	Processed	Staffed
Applied	Designed	Initiated	Procured	Standardized
Appointed	Determined	Inspected	Programmed	Started
Appraised	Developed	Inspired	Projected	Stimulated
Approved	Devised	Installed	Promoted	Streamlined
Arranged	Directed	Instituted	Proposed	Structured
Assembled	Discovered	Instructed	Proved	Submitted
Assessed	Dispatched	Insured	Provided	Suggested
Assigned	Distributed	Integrated	Published	Summarized
Assisted	Doubled	Interviewed	Purchased	Supervised
Attained	Earned	Invented	Quantified	Supported
Avoided	Edited	Inventoried	Realized	Surpassed
Brought	Effected	Invested	Reconciled	Sustained
Briefed	Employed	Investigation	Recruited	Tailored
Broadened	Empowered	Launched	Redesigned	Taught
Built	Encouraged	Led	Reduced	Tightened
Calculated	Endowed	Lightened	Regulated	Traded
Captured	Enforced	Located	Referred	Trained
Centralized	Enlisted	Made	Reinforced	Transacted
Clarified	Engineered	Maintained	Rejected	Transferred
Classified	Established	Managed	Related	Transformed
Coached	Estimated	Originated	Renegotiated	Trimmed
Collaborated	Fulfilled	Overcame	Renovated	Tripled

Your Name

Permanent Address
Home mailing address
Town, State, ZIP
Telephone

Email Address

Current Address
School address
Town, State, ZIP
Telephone

OBJECTIVE: Create a concise, powerful 1-2 line statement of purpose to give the resume a clear focus.

PROFILE: State interpersonal skills you possess
State any outstanding qualities you possess
State any functional skills you possess
State here if willing to relocate

EDUCATION:

Name of college: Town, State
Degree   Graduation date
Major:
Minor: Cumulative GPA: (if 3.0 or higher)
Optional: state percent of earned college expense

RELATED COURSES: *(Optional)*
List significant courses that add to your marketability (only upper level)

AWARDS & ACTIVITIES:

(List any of the following that you participated in)
Honors: *(List here if you received any academic honors)*
College Awards   Year-Year
Honor Societies   Year-Year
College Clubs   Year-Year
Offices Held   Year-Year
College Sports   Year-Year

EXPERIENCE:

Company: City, State (include country if outside the US)
State position title   *Dates of employment*
Describe job duties using action verbs
List most relevant tasks first; use an accomplishment focus
Use past tense for previous positions and present tense for current positions

COMPUTER SKILLS: *(optional)*
State any computer skills you may have.

INTERESTS: *(optional)*
List any personal interests, extensive travel, or language fluency you may have.

REFERENCES: (optional)
State that references will be provided upon request.

Jane A. Doe

Permanent Address
21 Bison Road
Worcester, MA 01600
555-555-5555

jadoe@nichols.edu

Current Address
Nichols College, Box 1
Dudley, MA 01571
555-555-5555

OBJECTIVE: Dedicated marketing student seeking an entry-level public relations position.

PROFILE: Poised and professional, with 3 years of client service experience
Thrive in a dynamic & challenging environment
Fluent in French and Spanish
Willing to relocate

EDUCATION:

Nichols College: Dudley, MA
Bachelor of Science in Business Administration   Expected May 2006
Major: Finance   Minor: Economics   GPA: 3.25

AWARDS & ACTIVITIES:

Dean's High Honors List and Dean's List
Who's Who in American Colleges   2005
Class Treasurer   2003-2006
NCAA Div. III, Field Hockey   2003-2005

EXPERIENCE:

John Hancock   Worcester, MA
Financial Assistant Intern   *2005-present*
- Accurately perform account analysis and database work.
- Provide support and information to shareholders about mutual funds.
- Answer client inquiries regarding balance information and fund features.
- Perform various administrative duties for Financial Advisors.

Commerce Bank & Trust Company   Webster, MA
Audit Operations Clerk   *2003-present*
- Assisted in coordinating a bank-wide contingency plan for operations.
- Implemented current IRS policy and regulations.
- Trained 5 staff members in current IRS procedures.
- Performed audits of various departments.

The Gap, Inc.   Marlboro, MA
Sales Associate   *Summers 2004, 2005*
- Sell fashionable apparel to customers.
      *Consistently exceed quarterly sales quota by at least 25%
- Responsible for updating and maintaining inventory records.
- Assist the managers with balancing daily cash and credit transactions.

REFERENCES: Furnished upon request.

E-RESUMES

Types of Resumes

An electronic resume is essential in today's job search, with over 80 percent of employers using the Web for recruiting purposes. Your resume needs to be formatted to fit the employer's needs to ensure that you don't miss out on valuable opportunities. Understanding how to develop and use an e-resume is an important aspect of your job search process.

First, there are several types of resumes which college students need in the job search process:
Paper Resumes – the traditional resume which can be mailed to a company or carried to an interview.

- design-focused with creative formatting
- unique, professional looking font; usually 11-12 font size
- creative, professional looking symbols
- columns are acceptable
- items can be left, right or center-margined
- "action words" (verbs) are used to describe work experience
- one page in length

Scannable Resumes - "The Plain Jane resume" - a basic version of the paper resume, without dividing lines and complex symbols. Scannable resumes need to be void of characters and features that could distort the original format when scanned. This type of resume should be used if your resume may be scanned at a company for distribution to hiring managers or stored in a database. A scannable resume can be on paper or electronic.

- text-focused in a plain format
- use easy-to-read font, ex.: Arial, Helvetica, Courier; 11-14 font
- use only symbols found on the keyboard (i.e. asterisk instead of bullets)
- eliminate underlining, italics, and graphics; bolding is usually acceptable
- no columns
- items can be left, right or center-margined
- keywords (nouns) in separate "Summary of Qualifications" section or buried in the text
- do not fold resume
- one page in length
- use only white or off white paper; print in black ink using a high quality laser printer
- do not send the resume as an attachment (unless instructed to do so) – it may not be opened by the company for fear of a virus or their software may not be able to open it. Always include a short (1-2 paragraph cover letter) followed by the resume in the body of the email.

ASCII or Text Resumes – The text resume is often referred to as the "ugly duckling" resume since it is an extremely plain, non-formatted document, with no room for creativity. The benefit of this electronic resume is that it is easily read by a variety of software programs. It is, in essence, the lowest common denominator of all formats and thus can be interpreted by most computerized systems.

- most often in electronic form
- text-focused in a plain format; stay within 65 characters per line but don't hit "enter" to start a new line, instead set your margins accordingly
- use easy to read font such as Arial, Helvetica, Courier; usually 11-14 font
- use only symbols found on the keyboard (i.e. asterisk instead of bullets)
- eliminate underlining, bullets, lines, italics, bold, underlines, shading, and graphics; use capitalization for headings; do not use parenthesis or brackets, even around telephone numbers; keyboard characters are acceptable: ==== or ++++ or ~~~ can be used to make rule lines; and *** or --- (hyphens) or oooo (lower-case o's) can be used in lieu of bullets
- no columns
- all items must be left-margined; your name goes on the first line with nothing else on that line
- keywords (nouns) in separate "Summary of Qualifications" section or buried in the text; use industry "buzz" words
- length should be reasonable but is not measured in pages
- the text resume is only meant for emailing or pasting onto a web site when requested; this resume is never meant to be printed on paper

HTML or Web resumes – These resumes are for the more IT-sophisticated applicant. A Web resume exists on a web page. Creativity is paramount here. First, a web resume demonstrates IT knowledge and expertise, and second, it can describe the applicant in greater detail as graphics, pictures and other information are easily assessable by links within the resume. The benefits of a web resume are: attractive appearance, no formatting issues, availability 24/7, easily expandable, demonstrates IT knowledge and creativity. The link to the web page can be included in the cover letter.

Using Keywords

Most often an electronic resume is saved in some type of a database for retrieval at another time. Resumes are later found in the database by someone conducting a query, or a search, using the "key words" search method. A recruiter may type in a word or phrase representing an important aspect of an open position. Only resumes which include the key word or phrase will appear. It is essential that your resume have many "key words" or "buzz words" appropriate to the position you are applying for, otherwise it will remain buried in the database.

Key words should be typed within the text of a resume. It is sometimes advised to include a section entitled "Key Words" near the bottom of the resume; however, be sure you possess experience and/or skills applicable to each key word you include.

How do you know which words to include? Key words should include your technical expertise, management skills, industry knowledge, education and training, geographic location and employment history. The best way to determine industry-specific keywords is to carefully read the job description for the position you are applying for and repeat back some of those words. Other sources for key words include: read newspapers for ads for similar positions, notice industry-specific lingo being used in professional chat rooms, attend conferences and seminars relative to the industry, ask people on the "inside", check The Occupational Outlook Handbook (in Career Services or online), note the company's mission statement, read trade publications, read annual reports, conduct an informational interview, use search engines (i.e. Google), go to sites such as www.babylon.com.

Submitting your resume
Company Websites
Many companies require you to apply online on their website. Each company develops its own process so be sure you understand what they expect from you. Two companies, Pfizer and Johnson and Johnson, stand out for the ease of applying on their website and for the related information they share with prospective employees. Check out their websites at:

www.pfizer.com/are/careers/mn_faqs_campus.html and www.jnj.com/student_resources/index.htm.

Public Job Search Websites
Hundreds of career websites exist for you to find and apply for positions. Their resume requirements vary. Monster.com and their subsidiary, www.monsterTRAK.com (the college-focused site), both allow you to upload a resume in any format or style you choose. Other sites are more specific in their requirements. Some other outstanding sites include: www.collegegrad.com, www.flipdog.com, and www.hotjobs.com. A list of outstanding websites is available in the Office of Career Services or online at the OCS webpage: www.nichols.edu/ocs/. Click on "Career Websites".

No matter where you send your resume, make sure it reaches its intended target by doing your homework before you send it. Read the website carefully or call the Human Resources department of the company to ask how your resume will be processed. You can then decide the best format for submitting your resume for optimal results.

Resources
The following websites have helpful information regarding e-resumes:

www.quintcareers.com
www.reslady.com
www.easyjob.net
www.jobweb.com
www.medzilla.com
www.careerperfect.com
www.wetfeet.com

REFERENCES

Identify the Best References
Former/current employers and college professors make the best references. Both groups have had the opportunity to evaluate your work, attitude and ability to get along with others. Other key references include coaches, club advisors, and college staff members who know you well. You are also known by who you know. If you know key people in your town/area who are widely respected, ask them too. These might include politicians, company owners, and people with prestige and/or status in the business world.

Ask For Their Permission
Always request permission of the person to use their name. If they gave you permission to use their name any time, do not assume that means for life. Stay in contact with your references and update them on your status as an applicant. Give your reference a copy of your updated resume so they are aware of everything you have done. And very importantly, ask them what information they would like you to list – their home, work or cell telephone number? A personal or work email address?

Keep Your Contacts Informed
Let your contact know what types of positions you are applying for and when they may be contacted. You can also ask your reference to mention specific things about you – i.e. a special project you completed for a course or a group presentation, accomplishments on the job, etc. Your resume will be useful to your contact in understanding your background and accomplishments.

Include Details About Your References
When you list the references, give their full name, current title, current company name and location. If you knew them from a former company, you may want to list in parenthesis: (former Supervisor at ABC Corporation). Ask your contact what specific information they would like to have listed. Never assume you can give out telephone numbers without permission.

Contacts Not to Use
The people who will not help your cause include relatives, clergy, personal friends, and certainly, therapists. If you work for a business owned by a relative, try to locate a manager or person other than a relative at the company who can speak on your behalf.

Thank Your References
Always be sure to thank the people who help you along the way. Your references will be invaluable assets in the interview process. Keep them informed of your progress. The more you involve them by sharing information, the more committed they will be to your success as a candidate.

SAMPLE LIST OF REFERENCES

(To be taken on an interview and/or submitted upon request)

Jane Student

67 Sea Street • Hull, MA 02045 • 774-645-2786 • jane.student@nichols.edu

List of References:

Dr. Holly Jordan, Professor
Nichols College
hjordan@nichols.edu
508-213-8976

Christopher Wilson, Corporate Recruitment Manager
Stevens Consulting Co.
cwilson@stevens.com
508-983-8754

Antonio Sierra, Manager of Public Relations
Reebok
1895 JW Foster Blvd
Canton, MA
as@reebok.com
781-871-4089

Samantha Cooper, Head Soccer Coach
Nichols College
scooper@nichols.edu
508-213-2277

EMPLOYMENT LETTERS
Seven Basic Types of Letters

Each employment letter has its own function and should be used accordingly. Be sure to sign the originals and keep a copy for your recruiting binder.

1. **Application/ Cover Letter**: This letter should be used when replying to an advertisement or job posting. It should introduce you and your resume while demonstrating that your qualifications fit the requirements of the job. Review the position description and adapt your cover letter to the qualities they are looking for. Also, be sure to provide examples of how your skills fit their needs.

2. **Prospecting Letter**: The purpose of this letter is to prospect for possible vacancies within your occupation. This letter is typically used for long distance job searches. Instead of tailoring your letter to a specific position, as you would in a cover letter, focus more on broader occupational or organizational dimensions to state how your skills match the work environment.

3. **Networking Letter**: This letter is designed to generate informational interviews. This allows you to meet with individuals who can provide you with specific information about your intended career.

4. **Thank you Letter**: This letter is one of the most important letters written throughout the job search process, yet the most infrequently used. It is used to express appreciation, gratitude and to strengthen your candidacy. Typically, anyone who helps you in any way should receive a thank you letter. Thank you letters should be sent to each interviewer within 24 hours of an interview.

5. **Acceptance Letter**: Use this type of letter to confirm the terms of your employment and to reinforce the company's decision to hire you. Most often, an acceptance letter follows a phone conversation in which the offer and terms are discussed.

6. **Withdrawal Letter**: Once you have made a decision and accepted a position, you should inform all other employers of your decision. Withdrawing your employment application from other employers should express gratitude for their consideration. State your intent to go with another organization.

7. **Rejection Letter**: Candidates should state in writing their decision to decline employment that does not fit their career objectives and interest. Indicate that you have given the offer careful consideration and have decided not to accept. Also, be sure to thank the employer for their time and consideration of you as an employee.

EXAMPLE: COVER LETTER

Your Address
City, State, Zip

Date

Mr./Ms. First Name Last Name
Title
Company
Address
City, State Zip

Dear Mr./ Ms. Last Name:

Please accept my cover letter as an application for the Marketing Assistant position you have advertised on monster.com (or Worcester Telegram) on April 25, 2009. I am a well qualified candidate who can bring a great deal of knowledge and enthusiasm to this position.

As my résumé indicates, I will be graduating from Nichols College in May with a Bachelor of Science in Business Administration degree with a concentration in Marketing. Throughout the past four years, I have been a member of the Lacrosse team and was named Captain my senior year. These roles have allowed me to effectively develop and hone my teamwork and leadership skills. I have also been a member of the Campus Activities Board (CAB) since my sophomore year. As part of the CAB team, I worked closely with other students to plan, organize and promote campus activities for over 100 events a year.

I have also held a part-time teller position in a local bank and have had the opportunity to learn many aspects of the banking industry. Some of my responsibilities have included responding to customer inquiries, promoting services offered by the bank, and gathering demographic data on customers to be used for our new marketing campaign. The marketing campaign proved to be fruitful as we increased annual sales by 10%. My experience as a bank teller has given me the interpersonal skills and technical skills needed for your marketing position.

I am a hardworking, motivated individual who would be an invaluable asset to your institution. During the course of my college career, I have maintained at 3.7 cumulative GPA and earned positions on several national honor societies. My strong desire to persevere even in challenging situations has afforded me success in a variety of arenas.

Please consider my cover letter and resume as a request for a personal interview to discuss my qualifications and your expectations in more detail. I will be contacting you during the week of (date) to determine if we can find a mutually convenient time to meet. In the meantime, I can be reached by phone at 123-4567 and via email at abcd@efgh.com. I look forward to meeting with you.

Sincerely,

Sign Name Here

Type Name Here

SAMPLE: PROSPECTING LETTER

Your Name
Address
City, State, Zip

Date

Mr./ Ms. Contact Name
Title
Company
Address
City, State Zip

Dear Mr./ Ms. Last Name:

After reading your company's description in CPC's Job Choices in Business, I would like to inquire about employment opportunities in your management training program. With a passion to work in retail management and a strong desire to relocate to the Boston area, I am interested to know more about your organization.

In May, I will receive my Bachelor of Science in Business Administration. My interest in business started in Junior Achievement while in high school and developed further through a variety of sales and retail positions throughout college. My internship with a large department store convinced me to pursue a career in retail. When I researched the top retailers in Boston, your company emerged as having a strong market position, an excellent training program, and a reputation for excellent customer service. In short, you provide the kind of professional retail environment I seek.

My education and experience match the qualifications you seek in your management trainees, but they do not tell the whole story. I know from customer and supervisor feedback that I have the interpersonal skills and motivation needed to build a successful career in retail management. My relatively extensive experience gives me confidence in my career direction and in my ability to perform competently.

While you must be busy this time of year, I would appreciate a few minutes of your time. I will call you during the week of (date) to discuss employment possibilities. In the meantime, if you would like to contact me, my number is (123) 456-7890 and my email address is first.last@college.edu.

Thank you very much for considering my request. I look forward to speaking with you soon.

Sincerely,

Sign Name Here

Type Name Here

SAMPLE: NETWORKING LETTER

Your Name
Address
City, State, Zip

Date

Mr./Ms. Contact Name
Title
Company
Address
City, State Zip

Dear Mr./ Ms. Last Name:

During a recent discussion with Dr. Jones, a professor of Accounting at Nichols College, I expressed interest in (accounting firm) and he suggested that I contact you. Dr. Jones thought that you would be in an excellent position, as a graduate of Nichols, to assist me with a career decision.

As an Accounting major in my junior year at Nichols College, I have begun to explore my career options. Last summer, I completed an internship in Public Accounting at ABC Company and am especially interested in becoming a CPA. Management Accounting and IRS work are also of interest to me, mainly due to the knowledge I have gained through classroom application and research.

Should your schedule permit, I would welcome the opportunity to meet with you to discuss the long term career implications of each path. I would also appreciate your insight into the day to day operations of a CPA.

I will be contacting you next week to set up a brief meeting at your convenience. In the meantime, I can be reached at (123) 456-7890. Thank you for considering my request.

Sincerely,

Sign Name Here

Type Name Here

SAMPLE: THANK YOU LETTER

Your Name
Address
City, State, Zip

Date

Mr./ Ms. Contact Name
Title
Company
Address
City, State Zip

Dear Mr./ Ms. Last Name:

I wish to thank you for speaking with me yesterday in regards to the Staff Accountant position within your firm. I enjoyed meeting you and learning more about your firm and clients.

My enthusiasm for the position and my interest in working for your firm were strengthened as a result of the interview. The quality of your company and employees is exceptional. The information you gave me yesterday regarding the company's goals and needs is just what I have been looking for. After visiting your firm, I am even more confident that my education and internship experiences fit your job requirements.

To reiterate, I have a strong interest in the position and in working with you and your staff. I know that I can make significant contributions to the firm. Please feel free to contact me at (123)-456-7890 if I can provide you with any additional
information.

Thank you again for your time and consideration.

Sincerely,

Sign Name Here

Type Name Here

SAMPLE: ACCEPTANCE LETTER

Your Name
Address
City, State, Zip

Date

Mr./ Ms. Contact Name
Title
Company
Address
City, State Zip

Dear Mr./ Ms. Last Name:

Please receive this letter as my formal acceptance to your employment offer. This position provides exactly the kind of experience I had hoped to find. I am delighted to be joining you and your staff and am grateful for the opportunity you have given me.

As we discussed, I will report to work at 8:00 a.m. on May 23, 2005 and will have completed the medical examination and drug testing by the new employee orientation on May 24, 2005.

Thank you again for providing me with this opportunity. I am very excited to join your marketing team.

Sincerely,

Sign Name Here

Type Name Here

SAMPLE: WITHDRAWAL LETTER

Your Name
Address
City, State, Zip

Date

Mr./ Ms. Contact Name
Title
Company
Address
City, State Zip

Dear Mr./ Ms. Last Name:

I am writing to inform you that I am withdrawing my application for the Program Coordinator position with _____. As indicated in my interview with you, I have been exploring several employment possibilities. This week I was offered an administrative position with a local city government and after careful consideration, I decided to accept it. My decision to accept the other position was difficult since I truly value the quality of your school and the opportunities you offer.

Thank you very much for interviewing and considering me for your position. I enjoyed meeting you and learning about the innovative community programs you are planning. You have a fine school and I wish you and your staff well.

Sincerely,

Sign Name Here

Type Name Here

SAMPLE: REJECTION LETTER

Your Name
Address
City, State, Zip

Date

Mr. / Ms. Contact Name
Title
Company
Address
City, State Zip

Dear Mr. / Ms. Last Name:

Thank you for taking the time to meet with me for an interview last week. Your offer of the Marketing Assistant position was very much appreciated.

While the offer of working with you and your team is enticing, I must decline the offer. As you know, I have been actively interviewing and I have accepted a similar position in a neighboring town. You have an excellent marketing team and I appreciate the time you took to meet with me.

Thank you again and best wishes for your continued success.

Sincerely,

`Sign name here`

Type Name Here

NOTES

JUNIOR COURSE

Week #3: Professional Presentation/ Communication Skills

NOTES

INTRODUCTION TO THE INTERVIEW
Key Points to Consider

Proper Dress

How you dress can either enhance or ruin your chances of getting a job. You are always safe if dressed conservatively on an interview, even if a company has a casual dress code. A suit gives the impression that you will take the process seriously and present yourself in a professional manner.

Arrival Time

It is essential to be on time, be positive, and be prepared. (Be 10-15 minutes early. This gives you the opportunity to experience the company's culture.) Be pleasant to EVERYONE upon arrival. You can never be sure who will have input in the hiring decision. Always smile and shake hands with everyone.

Enthusiasm

It is easy to say you are interested, but you must also demonstrate it. Show your enthusiasm by:

> Looking at the interviewer and paying attention
> Nod and smile during the conversation and be genuinely interested
> Maintain good posture, leaning slightly forward in your chair

Speaking

Pay close attention to your grammar, enunciation, and articulation. Poor diction and bad grammar are often reasons potential employers reject applicants. Be sure to pronounce words correctly and speak clearly steering away from slang such as "ah," "ya know," and "uhm."

Be Straightforward

Do not be evasive. Accentuate the positive and leave negative remarks about others and mistakes behind. If a mistake is brought up or questioned, assume responsibility and indicate how you have learned from your mistakes and have the ability to overcome and improve them. Lastly, provide evidence. If you say you are skilled in a particular area, explain it. Make statements throughout the interview which you can backup. This is where your portfolio will come in handy!

HOW OTHERS VIEW YOU

I. **Projection**
What is projected to others comes from:
1. Inside your head – attitude & confidence
2. Outward appearance – your dress, posture, facial expression
3. Reflection of you as seen through the eyes of others – references
4. Image through the written word – resume, portfolio, correspondence

II. **Nonverbal Communication**
Non-verbal communication sends a message. Be sure to be firm yet honest in your projection of the following:
1. Posture
2. Hands
3. Handshake
4. Facial expression
5. Head movement
6. Eye contact
7. Miscellaneous gestures

III. **Etiquette**
Etiquette is manners, and more. You demonstrate respect and appreciation for the interviewer and the interview itself with proper etiquette.

1. Demonstrate respect to those with a higher position or who have more authority. Respect in the workplace is based on the military model - the higher the position, the more respect. Gestures based on age or gender are based on the social model and do not belong in the workplace.
2. Introduce yourself in 10 seconds or less. Plan this ahead, practice it.
3. Stand 3-5 feet from anyone you are speaking with. Do not invade their "personal space".
4. Introduce yourself and others to the new person joining your group, unless there is another clear leader.
5. Use your manners ("please" and "thank you") often.
6. Stick to non-controversial topics. Don't ask personal questions.
7. Learn the art of "schmoozing".
8. Don't sit until invited to do so.
9. Be an active listener.
10. Be cordial to *everyone* you meet. You don't know who knows who and who can influence the hiring decision.
11. Don't reveal secrets of your former employer.
12. Keep your technology in working order. Have a professional sounding message on your answering machine or voice mail.
13. Be early and prepared!

INTERVIEWING FACTS & FIGURES

I.   A first impression is formed in approximately how much time?

        _____

II.   In a study of adult face-to-face encounters, it was found that the listener forms an impression
        of the speaker based on what percent of the following characteristics?

              verbal message – what we say   _____%

              how we say it – speed, tone, volume,
                    inflection & vocal quality   _____%

              facial expression and body language   _____%

III.   The average time an interviewer spends reading a resume or
        cover letter: _____

ANSWERS TO INTERVIEWING FACTS & FIGURES:

I.   7 seconds

II.   7%
            38%
            55%

III.   10 seconds

BODY LANGUAGE
Your Actions Speak Louder Than Words

Non- verbal communication, or body language, is an important component of the message we convey to others. In fact, some studies show that non-verbal communication is far more important than the verbal message. It's not what you say, it's how you say it that matters. Your body language/movements send a clear message – be sure you send the right message during an interview!

You should practice good body language before an interview. During an interview, be sure to "check in" with your body to ensure you are consistently sending a positive message to the interviewer.

Overall Positive Presentation:
You can make a positive first impression within seconds of meeting the interviewer, before any words are spoken. In order to do this, everything must be in place to ensure that your impression is a positive one. Enter the room with your head erect and your shoulders back, making sure your walking pace is lively. Make eye contact with the interviewer, raise your eyebrows slightly, and most importantly, you need to smile!

Handshake:
While consistent eye contact is important, so is a strong hand shake. To be sure to accomplish this, take your eyes off of the interviewer for just a split second before your hands meet to ensure you are getting a solid grip.
The hands should meet "web to web" before closing.
The handshake needs to be firm (but not overpowering), demonstrating confidence. One or two pumps are appropriate, using just one hand.

Facial Expression:
Portray energy and positivism: show a pleasant expression and smile often! Your smile does not need to be constant, just readily available.
Show that you are relaxed and confident: relax you facial muscles and jaw, avoid nervous twitches.

Hands:
Use your hands naturally while speaking. Some movement is good, just don't overdo it.
Keeping your hands visible during the interview sends a message that you are open and honest, likewise, keeping your hands consistently hidden may send an unconscious message that you have something to hide.

Eye Contact:
Good eye contact is essential for making a positive impression. You could have wonderful skills, excellent experience, and answer the questions well, but without maintaining good eye contact, you will quickly lose the opportunity to advance in the interview process.
Look into the interviewer's eyes most of the time but glance away occasionally so it won't appear that you are staring. Also, glance from one of the interviewer's eyes to the other periodically.
When looking away, be sure to look up - which will send a positive message, as if you are thinking and planning. A downward glance could send a message that you are not being straight-forward.

Other Movements:

Nodding your head in agreement sends a message that you are listening and involved in the conversation, but be sure to limit the nodding or it could be a distraction.

Try to keep most of your body still, refraining from nervous actions and twitches. A calm body demonstrates confidence.

Don't fold your arms across your body as it relays that you are defensive and/or you are not interested in the conversation.

In a chair, sit up straight and lean forward slightly. This shows interest.

If crossing your legs, point them toward the interviewer.

Occasionally expose your palms when speaking to show openness, friendliness and honesty. Don't overuse this.

Be professional, relax and enjoy the process!

Nonverbal Gestures	Interpretations
Arms Crossed	Defensiveness
Rubbing Hands	Anticipation
Open Palms	Sincerity, Openness
Patting/ Fondling Hair	Insecurity, Lack of Self Confidence
Tilted Head	Interest
Touching, Slightly Rubbing Nose	Rejection, Doubt, Lying
Brisk, Erect Walk	Confidence
Eye Contact	Confidence, Honesty

DRESSING FOR INTERVIEW SUCCESS
MEN

Preparing for a professional interview?
Follow the best modern/conservative dress guidelines for men

Suits

Conservative 2-piece business suit

Navy, medium blue, charcoal, and light gray are usually best

Shirts

Always wear a long-sleeved shirt

White, cream, or pale colored shirts are usually best

The paler and more subtle the shade, the better the impression you will form

Ties

Pure silk ties with a conservative pattern make the best professional impact

Tie should complement your suit. (The tie can range between 2 3/4" and 3 1/2" in width.)

When tied it should extend to your trouser belt

Shoes

Black or brown leather

STAY AWAY FROM OTHER MATERIALS AND COLORS

Socks

Socks should complement the suit; they should be blue, black, gray, or brown

Over-the-calf socks are the best

Accessories

The watch you wear should be simple & plain

Belts should match or complement the shoes you select

Jewelry

You may wear a wedding band, if applicable, and a small pair of cuff links

No earrings or other body jewelry

Overcoats

Professional looking overcoats in conservative colors

DRESSING FOR INTERVIEW SUCCESS
WOMEN

Preparing for a professional interview?
Follow the best modern/conservative dress guidelines for women

Suits

Always wear a suit with a jacket

Colors: Navy, charcoal, medium gray, black, and steel gray are usually best

Solid navy or gray with a white blouse would be the most professional and neatest

Blouses

Long sleeves will project a professional look

Solid colors and natural fabrics are best; white or cream are usually the most practical choices however, other soft colors can work, but should be worn only if it fully blends into your overall look.

Tuck in shirts

Shoes

Shoes should be leather: brown, black, navy, burgundy or forest green

Color of shoes should be the same or a darker tone than your skirt or slacks

Flats are okay; a shoe with a heel of up to about 2 1/2" is acceptable

Shoes should be closed-toe and not overly pointed

Stockings or Pantyhose

Neutral skin tones are the safest, most conservative choice

Wearing sheer white or cream pantyhose would be within the realm of professional etiquette if it complements your attire

Accessories

Use a professional looking briefcase instead of a purse. In addition to brown and burgundy, you may also include navy and black as possible colors for your case

Belts should match or complement the shoes you select

Jewelry

One set of earrings will be appropriate and no more than one ring on each hand

Limit other jewelry (i.e., one conservative necklace and watch. No bangle bracelets or other body jewelry)

Makeup

Minimal use of make-up

Use a clear or conservative nail polish

No perfume

JUNIOR COURSE

Week #4: Introduction to Interviewing

NOTES

INTERVIEWING SKILLS

Preparation – after mailing (a perfect) cover letter & resume
Put everything in place – appropriate voice mail, get ready for a call, outfit clean, references in order
Research company
Prepare for questions you will be asked and those to ask

Dress
Wear a conservative suit and shoes
No perfume/after shave
No smoking
Look at yourself in a mirror before entering

Telephone Skills
Plan ahead – what to say
Show enthusiasm in voice
Use your first and last name, reference how you know them
If they are busy, ask when you can call back
When leaving a voice mail:
>speak slowly
>keep short
>repeat name & telephone #

Arrival
Drive by the location the day before at the same time
Arrive 10-15 minutes early
Observe the environment while waiting, do not read
Treat everyone as the hiring person
Bring: folder with pad and pen, typed questions to ask, typed list of references, 2-3 copies of resume on resume paper
Smile!

Body Language
Entrance – good posture, look confident, smile
Handshake- look at hands just as gripping, firm shake
Posture in chair – sit up straight and lean forward slightly
Tone of voice – talk a little louder than you would with a friend
No gum or mints

Interview Tips
Be yourself, but professional
Turn off cell phone, better to leave in the car
Speak clearly and with enthusiasm
Be positive
Be honest

Be thorough – but no tangents
Be specific- give examples

Types of Interviews
- A. Informational
- B. Behavioral
- C. Structured
- D. Un-structured
- E. Panel of Candidates
- F. Panel of Interviewers
- G. Stress
- H. All day interview, lunch/meal etiquette

Second & Third Interviews
Questions you may be asked – more specific/task oriented
Hiring manager/supervisor is usually the interviewer

QUESTIONS TO EXPECT DURING AN INTERVIEW

Introductory Questions:
Tell me about yourself. (*It is best to keep your answer to this question short, about 1-2 minutes, offering answers that show your skills/qualities relevant to this specific position. You may want to express your degree, work experience, and strengths, both interpersonal as well as work-related.*)
Why did you apply for this position?
Tell me about your college and why you chose it.

Questions about Job Performance, Career Goals, and Experience:
Do you prefer working alone or in groups?
What is your long-term career objective?
What kind of job do you see yourself doing five years from now?
How does this position fit in with your overall career goals?
Everyone has strengths and weaknesses as workers. What are your strong points for this position? What would be a weakness?
What kind of people do you find it most difficult to work with? Why? How do you get around this?
What would you say is the most important thing you look for in a job?
If I were to ask your current (last) employer about your ability as a _____, what would s/he say?
Why should we hire you when we have candidates with more experience or better credentials?
What motivates you? How do you motivate others?
What qualifications do you have that make you think you will be a success here?
The person in this position needs to be (innovative) and (proactive). Can you describe some things you have done to demonstrate these qualities?
How do you react when you see co-workers disagreeing? Do you become involved or hold back?

Self-Assessment:
What things give you the greatest satisfaction?
Describe your most rewarding experience.
What things frustrate you the most? How do you cope with them?
Can you describe a difficult obstacle you have had to overcome? How did you handle it? How do you feel this experience affected your personality or ability?
If I were to ask your current (former) supervisor what your strengths are, what would he/she say? (*Give 2-3 strengths and give a brief example of each.*)

Questions to Make You Think:

What are your key weaknesses? (*Present one strength as a weakness, ex.: workaholic, pay too-close attention to detail, etc.OR mention a corrected weakness, ex.: I found I need to brush up my Microsoft Access skills, so I've enrolled in a class. Present ONE weakness and put a positive spin on it.*)

What do you think of your last boss? (*Be positive.*)

How would you deal with a high-strung personality?

How do I rate as an interviewer? (*Do not voice an ounce of criticism.*)

Situational/Behavioral Questions:

How would you deal with a difficult co-worker?

Describe a situation in a past position where you stepped up and took a leadership role.

If your supervisor told you to do something and you knew it was dead wrong, what would you do?

Give an example of a crisis situation you were involved in. What role did you play?

Five Questions You Most Likely Will Be Asked (be sure to prepare):

1) Tell me about yourself

2) What are your strengths?

3) What are your weaknesses?

4) Why do you want to work here?

5) Why should we hire you?

WORKSHEET OF DIFFICULT INTERVIEW QUESTIONS/ANSWERS

Directions: Identify difficult questions you may be asked in the interview. Write the question and your response. This is the time to anticipate and prepare.

Question: _____
Answer: _____
_____
_____

Question: _____
Answer: _____
_____
_____

Question: _____
Answer: _____
_____
_____

Question: _____
Answer: _____
_____
_____

Question: _____
Answer: _____
_____
_____

Question: _____
Answer: _____
_____
_____

Question: _____
Answer: _____
_____
_____

Question: _____
Answer: _____
_____
_____

QUESTIONS TO ASK ON AN INTERVIEW

Candidate qualities. "What qualities are you looking for in a candidate?" "What qualities would it take to make someone successful in this position?"

Company culture/environment. "Every company seems to have its own culture (or environment). How would you describe the culture at this company?"

Work schedule. "Can you please tell me what a typical day would be like for a person in this position?"

Supervision. "Who would my direct supervisor be and what is his/her style of supervision?"

Training. "What is the training process like and how long would it be before I would be working on my own?" "Is there on-going training after the initial training period?"

People contact. "Who would I be interacting with on a daily basis? At other times?"

Evaluation. "How often would my performance be evaluated, and by whom?"

Advancement. "Is advancement possible beyond this position?" If so, "Given outstanding performance in this position, how long do expect someone would be in this position before advancement?"

Role within the company. "Can you please tell me how this position helps to contribute to the success of this company?"

State your desire for the position. "I am looking forward to this opportunity. What is the next step of the application process?"

Recap what you can offer. "To summarize, I am VERY interested in this position and believe my skills and experience in _____ would ensure my ability to help your company in its continued success."

Be sure to send a thank you letter within 24 hours of an interview!

ILLEGAL INTERVIEW QUESTIONS
And How to Respond

In the United States, there are several topics which interviewers should avoid asking you about since your response could lead to legal action against the employer. Employers are not allowed to discriminate against you on the basis of any of the following:

Age	**Race/ Ethnicity/ National Origin**
Family/Marital status	**Religion or Creed**
Disability	**Financial background/status**
Gender	**Sexual preference**

Questions about any of these topics are not always illegal to ask, however, if your response to any of these questions was a reason for not hiring you, then it would be considered discrimination and the basis for a possible lawsuit. Therefore, most qualified interviewers will not ask you questions regarding any of the topics.

There are some exceptions to this rule. Interviewers are able to ask questions regarding these factors if it directly relates to the position. For instance, you cannot be asked if you are in good physical condition. However, you can be asked if you are able to lift a 40 pound package up to 100 times in a shift if you were applying for a position that required this kind of physical labor. An interviewer cannot ask your age but they can ask if you are at least 18 years of age if you would be serving alcoholic beverages. The question must relate directly to the job requirements.

There are several ways you can respond to an illegal question in an interview:

Answer the Question
You can answer the question. You may run the risk of the information being used against you, but since most interviewers are not purposely seeking information to discriminate against you, you would appear cooperative and honest.

Ask about Relevance
The question may or may not be relevant to the job responsibilities. It is appropriate for you to ask the interviewer if s/he could explain how the information they seek relates to the position. They may not have been clear with their question, and very innocently asked it inappropriately. You could ask, "I'm a little confused by your question, could you please tell me how the information you seek is related to this position?"

Address the Need
You can try to understand the apparent need behind the question and respond to the need instead of answering the question. For instance, the interviewer may ask if you have a family. In all honesty, s/he may not really care if you have one, but they may worry that you might have limited evening and weekend hours you are available to work. You could answer the question, "If you are concerned that I may have limited hours to offer you beyond the regular office hours, please be assured that my

schedule is flexible and I am willing to work hard to do an outstanding job in this position." You can always follow that response with asking if you offered the information they were looking for.

Kindly Refuse to Answer

You can refuse to answer the question. You may state that you are uncomfortable answering it. You may also politely state that the question is not appropriate in the interview process, or that it is an illegal question. This response, while within your legal rights, may turn off the interviewer, particularly if the question wasn't intended to offend. If you choose this response, be sure it is carefully worded so you don't seem uncooperative or confrontational.

Remember, most interviewers will never purposely ask you an illegal question. If they do ask one, it most likely means they haven't been trained about the legality of interviewing or they are just trying to innocently make conversation. You have options for responding to these types of questions. However, if you feel an interviewer is asking illegal questions and uses the information to discriminate against you, you may want to contact the local Equal Opportunity Office for assistance.

ILLEGAL QUESTIONS?

The following questions were typically asked at job interviews in the 1970's. Can you pick out the questions that are now illegal for employers to ask according to Equal Employment Opportunity Act?

1. What traits / characteristics do you think you need in order to be successful in this position?
2. What is your five/ ten year plan?
3. Do you attend church/ synagogue on Sundays?
4. Why did you choose Nichols College?
5. Are you married?
6. When did you first contribute to family income?
7. Do you prefer to work alone or in groups?
8. What are your strengths?
9. How serious is your current relationship?
10. Tell me about yourself
11. I noticed that your GPA is not over a 3.0, do you have a learning disability?
12. What are your weaknesses?
13. Where were you born?
14. Can you elaborate more on your past experience as a _____?
15. What type of people do you have a hard time working with?
16. What interests you about our organization?
17. Is this your maiden or married name?
18. Do you have young children or plan to have children soon?
19. What is the most important thing you look for in a position?
20. What motivates you?
21. When did you graduate from high school?
22. What do you like to do in your spare time?
23. What is your father's occupation?
24. Why did you leave your last job?
25. Describe a time where you took on a leadership role?
26. How would you prefer to be supervised?
27. Are your parents still married?
28. Were you ever in the military?
29. How would you rate your communication skills?
30. If I asked your boyfriend/ girlfriend to describe you, what would s/he say?
31. What is your greatest accomplishment?
32. What percentage of your college education were you responsible for?
33. What made you decide to major in___?
34. What do you think of your last boss?
35. How do you feel about having quarterly performance appraisals?
36. Do you believe in interracial marriage?
37. If there is one thing you could change about yourself, what would it be and why?
38. Do you have any plans to continue your education?
39. What interests you most about this position?

NOTES

JUNIOR COURSE

Week #5: Interviewing In-depth

NOTES

INTERVIEW TYPES AND METHODS

I. **Types of Interviews**

Informational

Behavioral

Stress

Focused

Screening

Situational

II. **Methods**

1 on 1

Candidate panel

Multiple interviewers

Structured/unstructured

Day-long

Meals

III. **Reality**

Employers don't always know what they want – qualities, skills, traits in a candidate

Most interviewers are the hiring manager and they most likely haven't received any training in how to properly interview a candidate

Interviewers want you to leave liking them and their company

Most interviewers don't want you to feel nervous; they will try to relax you

THE IMPORTANCE OF BUILDING RAPPORT

What is rapport?
A state of mutual trust and respect existing between people. Rapport is the primary basis for all successful communication.

Why is building rapport so important at the beginning of the interview? Building rapport puts both the interviewer and interviewee at ease. The interviewer builds rapport with you in order to make you feel comfortable and share information about yourself. You build rapport with the interviewer in order to get the interviewer to like you and to feel that you are a qualified candidate.

Developing Rapport
The first phase of rapport building lasts approximately five minutes, yet sets the tone for the remainder of the interview. Making a good first impression is crucial. The way you present yourself, your first remark, and the way you are dressed all make an impression on your interviewer. Make a conscious choice about how you present yourself.

Upon meeting the interviewer, you have already communicated a visual message. The next step in attaining rapport is to make a positioning statement which should include the interviewers name, your appreciation for the interview, and an indication that you are ready for the interview. For instance: "Mr. Smith, thank you for allowing me to interview with you today. I am excited to share my skills and qualifications with you."

Maintaining Rapport
Now that you have created rapport with your interviewer, it is necessary to maintain it. Many interviewers tend to focus on negative things. Something in your attitude or a naïve remark can have an effect on the good rapport you build. Some traits to stay away from include low confidence, arrogance and cockiness, overuse of humor, and over talking.

Ending with Rapport
After attaining and maintaining rapport, your next step will be to limit the end of the interview to a few topics in order to sustain the rapport built. If things have gone well and you know that the end is near, limit your questions to these topics: a reiteration that you really want this job, understanding the next step of the process, and a thank you for the interview.

KEEPING YOUR COOL IN AN INTERVIEW

Tips on how to stay cool, calm and collected during an interview

Be confident, but not arrogant, believe in yourself – confidence generates more confidence

Don't let the fear of failure overwhelm you

Relax your body then calm your emotions and thoughts

Trust yourself

Keep your hands open to let them air dry and not get sweaty

Believe in yourself and the interviewer will believe in you

The topic of an interview is you, and who knows you better than you?

Don't second guess your responses

Remember you're also interviewing the company to find out more about it and whether you will enjoy working there, to determine if you like the atmosphere, culture and people

Don't worry about possible rejection, think positive!

Prepare well in advance and relax before going to the interview

It's normal to be a little nervous before and at the start of the interview, just try to relax

Preparation will give you the advantage to know more about the company than they know about you, giving you the edge

Relax and enjoy the interview process; if you don't receive an offer it's ok

If the interviewer gives you feedback, accept it, but don't let a negative response lower your self-confidence; use the information to your advantage down the road

SILENCE IN THE INTERVIEW

How to use silence to your advantage

Silence initiated by the interviewer:

When silence is imposed by the interviewer it may be to develop a stressful situation to see how you will handle it, so relax and go with it for a brief period.

Break the silence only by asking a question.

Some interviewers are inexperienced and may pause for longer than expected because they don't know what to ask next. If this is the case, help them out by asking a question, such as "Would you like me to explain my last answer in more detail?" or "Could I give you an example of something I created in my _____ class which directly relates to this position?"

It is your responsibility to end the silence if it is not imposed as stress.

Silence initiated by the interviewee

Silence initiated by the interviewee can be seen as a sign of confidence.

Taking several seconds to think of a good answer before speaking works in your favor and may be appreciated by the interviewer. This shows that you can think before acting. However, do not overuse this.

When there is a period of silence, do not apologize, whisper or get defensive.

DO'S AND DO NOT'S OF INTERVIEWING

Things to Consider

Do's

Know exactly where the company is located and how long it will take you to get there
Research the company and job you are applying for
Dress the part
Plan to arrive ten to fifteen minutes early
Greet the receptionist with courtesy and respect
Bring extra résumés
Greet the interviewer by proper name, using Mr./Ms., until invited to use his/her first name
Shake hands firmly and make eye contact
Wait to be seated until offered
Show enthusiasm and display confidence
Avoid controversial topics
Show what you can do for the company rather than ask what they can do for you
Ask intelligent questions about the job, company, and industry
Close the interview by telling the interviewer you want the job and ask what the next step is
Write a thank you note to each interviewer within 24 hours

Do Not's

Ask about salary
Speak negatively about difficulty locating the office, travel arrangements, weather, or any topic
Say that you didn't get much sleep
Explain why you might do poorly in an interview
Volunteer why you lost your last job or make negative reference to anyone
Discuss personal or family issues
Chew gum or breath mints
Rely on your application or résumé to do the selling for you
Tell jokes
Be soft spoken
Lie or exaggerate
Answer yes or no; instead you should explain yourself
Answer a cellular phone, in fact, turn it off before the interview
Make reference to religion, politics, race, gender, age, or national origin
Try to butter up the interviewer by complimenting on appearance

CHECKING YOUR REFERENCES

Questions your interviewer may ask your personal references

How long has the candidate worked for you?

What was the quality of his/her work?

How much responsibility did s/he have?

How did s/he get along with others?

Did s/he require close supervision?

Was s/he prompt?

Why did s/he leave your company?

Do you know of anything that would disqualify him/her for the job we're considering hiring him/her for?

Can you think of anything I should know about him/her that I haven't already asked?

Do you know of anyone else with whom I may speak about him/her?

Would you hire this individual again? Why or why not?

Remember, always ask if you can use someone as a reference – do not assume. When you solicit someone to be a reference, you should keep them informed. When applying for a position, make sure your reference has a copy of your resume and the job description.

People to ask can include:

Professors
Employers
Former Employers
Internship Supervisor
Advisors
Coaches
College Staff Member

MOCK INTERVIEWS

INTERVIEW ORDER AND REQUIREMENTS

I. ORDER OF INTERVIEWS

Interviewer-*Week 6*/**Interviewee-***Week8*   **Interviewee-** *Week 6*/**Interviewer-***Week 8*

Pair#

#1   1. _____   2. _____

#2   3. _____   4. _____

#3   5. _____   6. _____

#4   7. _____   8. _____

#5   9. _____   10. _____

Interviewer-*Week 7*/**Interviewee-***Week 9*   **Interviewee-***Week 7*/**Interviewer-***Week 9*

#6   11. _____   12. _____

#7   13. _____   14. _____

#8   15. _____   16. _____

#9   17. _____   18. _____

#10   19. _____   20. _____

II. ITEMS TO SUBMIT LAST DAY OF MOCK INTERVIEWS: (must be typed, neat, include name)

Items to be submitted in folder:

1) Interviewer questions for interviewee (min. 15)
2) Company/Position Information Form (research/summary of company *in your own words*)
3) Interviewee questions for interviewer (min. 8)
4) Revised cover letter for mock interview position on resume paper
5) Revised resume on resume paper
6) Thank you letter for interviewer

NOTES

MOCK INTERVIEWS

Interviewer Questions for Interviewee
(these must be typed and turned in)

Date of interview: _____

Interviewer: _____   Interviewee: _____

Type of interview to be conducted: _____

Questions:

1.

2.

3.

4.

5.

6.

7.

8.

9.

10.

11.

12.

13.

14.

15.

NOTES

MOCK INTERVIEWS

Interviewee Questions for Interviewer

Date of interview: _____

Interviewee: _____   Interviewer: _____

Questions:

1.

2.

3.

4.

5.

6.

7.

8.

NOTES

MOCK INTERVIEWS

Company/Position Information Form
(to be completed by mock interviewee and typed in your own words – not copied from a website)

Date of Mock Interview: _____

Interviewee: _____   Interviewer: _____

Company Information:

Name of (real) Company:

Company Location(s):

Company Profile: type of business/organization and product(s) or service(s) rendered:

Position Information:

Title of entry-level position interviewing candidate for (real or fictitious position):

Other pertinent information:

NOTES

JUNIOR COURSE

Weeks #6-9 Mock Interviews

NOTES

MOCK INTERVIEWS

Interviewee Feedback Form

Interviewee: _____

	Practice Needed		Good		Excellent	
Personal Presentation	1	2	3	4	5	
Attitude	negative 1	2	3	4	5	positive
Communication Skills	1	2	3	4	5	
Professionalism	1	2	3	4	5	
Quality of Answers	1	2	3	4	5	
Body Language	1	2	3	4	5	
Interview Overall	1	2	3	4	5	

Comments:

NOTES

JUNIOR COURSE

Week # 10: Draft Portfolio Review Session

NOTES

PORTFOLIO PEER EVALUATION FORM

Portfolio Belongs To: _____

Evaluator: _____

1. Please rate the quality of the contents in the portfolio:

		Not Applicable	Poor		Good		Excellent
Required Categories	Career & Professional Planning/Growth	N/A	1	2	3	4	5
	Teamwork/Leadership Skills	N/A	1	2	3	4	5
	Communication Skills	N/A	1	2	3	4	5
	Analytical/Problem Solving/Critical Thinking	N/A	1	2	3	4	5
	Technology Related Skills	N/A	1	2	3	4	5
Optional Categories	Arts/Cultural	N/A	1	2	3	4	5
	Volunteer Experience/Community Service	N/A	1	2	3	4	5
	Other	N/A	1	2	3	4	5

Additional Required Items

_____ Cover with Name
_____ Table of Contents
_____ Introductory Statement
_____ Resume
_____ Letter of Reference

Comments:

	No		Somewhat		Yes
2. Does the portfolio look professional? *Please explain:*	1	2	3	4	5
3. Is the portfolio organized and in a logical order? *Please explain:*	1	2	3	4	5
4. Did the student present the portfolio in a clear and understandable manner? *Please explain:*	1	2	3	4	5

Comments:

JUNIOR COURSE

Week # 11: Post-Graduation Options/ Graduate School/Multiculturalism

NOTES

APPLYING TO GRADUATE SCHOOL

Researching Prospective Schools

Begin your research early in your junior year; most graduate degree deadlines occur before December of the prior year

Talk to faculty members in your chosen field to determine the appropriate graduate degree for your career path.

Visit websites such as www.gradschools.com and www.petersons.com to find and research schools and degree programs; use the DISCOVER program in OCS (located in the "informational" side under "Search"); or use the resources in the OCS library.

Email or call recommended institutions for information including course catalogs, faculty listings, specializations, fellowships, assistantships and scholarships.

Visit prospective schools to meet with faculty members and graduate students.
> Talk to current graduate students in your field. Ask the Office of Career Services (OCS) to help you locate graduate students.

Components of an Application

Standardized Tests
> Most graduate programs require tests such as the GRE, GMAT, or LSAT. Take these tests in the spring of your Junior year for admission in the fall after you graduate (especially if you like to practice).Scores typically take about 6 weeks
> from the test date to be delivered.

Letters of Recommendation
> Request letters of recommendation far in advance of your due date. Provide the faculty member with a copy of your resume and personal statement.
> Only request letters of reference from faculty members who will be able to provide an in-depth recommendation based upon your academic performance. (Some business degree programs may request letters from employers/ supervisors).

Resume
> Have your resume professionally critiqued by OCS.

Personal Statement/Essay(s)
> Allot considerable time and give plenty of forethought to your personal statement. Most applications ask for you to state a clear focus for your future.
> Write several drafts, seeking advice from a faculty advisor and/or the writing lab. The essay takes on even greater importance if your GRE/GMAT scores and GPA do not reflect your ability because it gives you an opportunity to explain your academic background.
> Read the instructions carefully and adhere to all stated deadlines.

Transcripts
> Make sure that you can get official transcripts from your undergraduate institutions. (You may not be able to get transcripts if you have unpaid parking tickets or overdue library books).

Costs of Applying

Application fees (typically about $40/school) are usually non-refundable.

Universities and colleges charge fees for sending transcripts ($2-$10/transcript) and many graduate institutions request two with your application.

Test costs: the GMAT costs $250; the GRE costs $130 (additional subject tests may be required); the LSAT costs $118.

Submitting Applications

Deadlines vary according to school, so check your application. Complete your applications early since financial support decisions typically are made early in the calendar year.

Evaluating Offers of Admission

Talk to a faculty member in your chosen field.
Consider the quality of the academic program—what will a degree from institution X be worth in the job market?
Which institution will serve your needs best?
Where is your best offer of financial support?

Benefits

Individuals who hold a master's degree usually earn over $300,000 more during their lifetime than an individual with a bachelor's degree. And, doctoral and professional graduates tend to earn about $800,000 more over their lifetime than a bachelor's graduate.

As you begin your search for a graduate school, you have the privilege of entering into coursework that is of interest to you. Make sure you choose a school where you can focus on what interests you the most.

Considerations

Keep in mind that when you enter into graduate school, it is a lot more focused than your undergraduate degree. You should have a good idea of the career path and subjects you want to pursue. If you are unsure of what you want to do, try the workplace first. Explore some of your options before diving into graduate school.

Grad school will be a lot more demanding than your undergraduate degree. You will be much more focused on a certain topic and constant reading will be required. If you enjoy reading into the middle of the night or debating issues related to your degree than grad school is the place for you.

CAREER SEARCH PROCESS:
Industry/Position/Salary/Location

Please check off all items that you would consider for an entry-level position/career:

Industry Type:

__ Accounting and Management Consulting

__ Advertising, marketing, and Public Relations

__ Aerospace

__ Apparel, Fashion, and Textiles

__ Architecture, Construction, and Engineering

__ Arts and Entertainment

__ Automotive

__ Banking/Savings and Loans

__ Biotechnology, Pharmaceutical, and Scientific R&D

__ Business Services and Non-Scientific Research

__ Charities and Social Services

__ Chemicals/Rubber and Plastics

__ Communications:

     Telecommunications and Broadcasting

__ Computer Hardware, Software, and Services

__ Educational Services

__ Electronic/Industrial Electrical Equipment

__ Environmental and Waste Management Services

__ Fabricated/Primary Metals and Products

__ Financial Services

__ Food and Beverages/Agriculture

__ Government

__ Health Care: Services, Equipment, Products

__ Hotels and Restaurants

__ Insurance

__ Legal Services

__ Manufacturing: Misc. Consumer

__ Manufacturing: Misc. Industrial

__ Mining/Gas/Petroleum/Energy Related

__ Paper and Wood Products

__ Printing and Publishing

__ Real Estate

__ Retail

__ Sports and Recreation

__ Stone, Clay, Glass, and Concrete Products

__ Transportation/Travel

__ Utilities: Electric/Gas/Water

__ Misc. Wholesaling

Salary:

__ up to $19,999	__ $60,000 – 64,999
__ $20,000 – 24,999	__ $65,000 – 69,999
__ $25,000 – 29,999	__ $70,000 – 74,999
__ $30,000 – 34,999	__ $75,000 – 79,999
__ $35,000 – 39,999	__ $80,000 – 84,999
__ $40,000 – 44,999	__ $85,000 – 89,999
__ $45,000 – 49,999	__ $90,000 – 94,999
__ $50,000 – 54,999	__ $95,000 – 99,999
__ $55,000 – 59,999	__ $100,000+

Location:

____ New England:
    __ Connecticut   __ New Hampshire
    __ Maine   __ Rhode Island
    __ Massachusetts   __ Vermont

__ New Jersey   __ New York

__ Virginia/ Washington DC   __ Pennsylvania

__ Florida   __ Other: _____

Other Factors Influencing Your Decision:

_____
_____
_____
_____
_____
_____
_____
_____
_____
_____

CAREER SEARCH PROCESS: Self Choice

Name: _____

1) At work I prefer:

|_____|_____|_____|_____|_____|_____|_____|
High people contact   Low people contact

2) At work I prefer:

|_____|_____|_____|_____|_____|_____|_____|
Individual work/projects   Team work/projects

3) Where I want to work: Where I want to live:

_____ Urban   _____ Urban
_____ Suburban   _____ Suburban
_____ Country   _____ Country

Examples: _____   Examples: _____
_____   _____
_____   _____
_____   _____

4) The kinds of tasks I like to perform (prioritize 1- first choice, 2- second choice, etc.):

_____ Creative/artistic expression   _____ Coordinate projects with others
_____ Manual/physical labor   _____ Supervise people
_____ Train/demonstrate to others   _____ Manipulate tools
_____ Make public presentations   _____ Writing/narrative work
_____ Problem solving   _____ Hands-on work/handle materials
_____ Make decisions   _____ Numerical/analytical work
_____ Investigative work   _____ Sales
_____ Research   _____ Other: _____

5) I prefer to work with (prioritize 1- first choice, 2 – second choice, etc.):

_____ People   _____ Animals
_____ Office/paper   _____ Food/beverage
_____ Machinery/equipment   _____ Computers/software
_____ Manufactured products   _____ Medicine/chemicals/biological materials
_____ Other: _____   _____ Other: _____

Comments:

CAREER SEARCH PROCESS

Questions About My Job

1) Beginning with your most recent employment, describe *in detail* each job you had. Include in this summary your title, company, responsibilities, salary, achievements and successes, failures, and reason for leaving.

2) How would you change anything in your job history if you could?

3) In your career so far, what responsibilities have you enjoyed most? Why?

4) What kind of job do you think would be a perfect match for your talents and interests?

5) What responsibilities do you want to avoid?

6) How hard are you prepared to work?

7) If you want the top job in your field, are you prepared to pay the price?

8) What have your subordinates thought about you as a boss? As a person?

9) What have your superiors thought about you as an employee? As a person?

10) Can your work make you happier? Should it?

11) If you have ever been fired from any job, what was the reason?

12) How long do you want to work before retirement?

CAREER SEARCH PROCESS:
Occupation Research Form

Name: _____

1)   Occupation/Job Title: _____
        Type of Industry: _____
        Location: _____
        Description of Work/Job Tasks: _____

        _____

        _____

        _____

        _____

        Personal Qualities Required: _____

        _____

        Education or Training Required: _____

        _____

        Employment Outlook/Future Opportunities: _____

        _____

        Salary Range: _____
        Source(s) of Information: _____

2)   Occupation/Job Title: _____
        Type of Industry: _____
        Location: _____
        Description of Work/Job Tasks: _____

        _____

        _____

        _____

        _____

        Personal Qualities Required: _____

        _____

        Education or Training Required: _____

        _____

Employment Outlook/Future Opportunities: _____

_____

_____

Salary Range: _____

Source(s) of Information: _____

3)   Occupation/Job Title: _____

Type of Industry: _____

Location: _____

Description of Work/Job Tasks: _____

_____

_____

_____

_____

Personal Qualities Required: _____

_____

_____

Education or Training Required: _____

_____

_____

Employment Outlook/Future Opportunities: _____

_____

_____

Salary Range: _____

Source(s) of Information: _____

MULTICULTURALISM IN THE WORKPLACE

It's no secret that the United States prides itself on having one of the strongest and still growing economies, and is a world superpower. Yet, the continued success of the United States economy is based more and more on business relationships that are being formed with successful companies all over the world. With the increased focus on internationalism, the United States now depends on businesses and the economy in other cultures to maintain its status.

Chances are that no matter what career path you choose in life, you will at some point interact with someone from another culture. Learning business cultural etiquette is not only respectful but it is the key to long term business success. No one country conducts business exactly the same as another. Researching and studying these cultures will demonstrate respect to others and is essential in order to close the business deal.

What many Americans may not understand is that even the littlest gesture, such as using the okay sign, can be extremely offensive in another culture. Demonstrating respect may be as easy as learning a few words in a different language or as hard as having to change one's behavior. Regardless, the end result will be good for business.

The following pages outline some of the cultural and business etiquette expected in other cultures. These five countries show a variety of cultural protocols but by no means are the only ones. These countries were selected to demonstrate variety and represent the thousands of cultural possibilities across the globe.

Business Culture in Brazil

DRESS
- Business dress is casual. You may wear jeans and a nice shirt to a meeting and would be totally accepted.

BODY LANGUAGE / GESTURES
- Expect long hand shakes
- Women will often kiss cheeks
- Touching will occur during a conversation
- The O.K sign is considered vulgar
- Maintain eye contact at all times
- People may stand closely in front of each other when talking

LANGUAGE / ADDRESSING OTHERS
- Portuguese is the dominant language
  - They take offense if you address them in Spanish
- Brazilians are likely to be very fast talkers
- They may interrupt often
- Never use the phrase "In America", they consider themselves Americans as well
- Do not use a first name unless invited to do so
- Use professional titles such as Doctor or Professor.
  - Those without titles use "Senhor" or "Senhora"
- People usually have two surnames.
  - The mothers surname comes before the fathers surname

HOW BUSINESS IS CONDUCTED

- Will only do business through connections
- Expect long term business relationship
- Hire a Brazilian contact to make connections if you do not already have one
- Make appointments at least two weeks in advance
  - Showing up without an appointment is unacceptable
- Schedule appointments between 10am and noon or 3:00pm and 5:00pm
  - Give yourself two to three hours between each meeting
  - Official business hours are 8:30am – 5:30pm
- Being late for meetings is a part of the culture. Expect to wait around. Yet, you should always be on time.

CULTURALLY UNIQUE

- Giving gifts is appropriate
  - Offer to buy lunch or dinner
  - Do not give anything that is obviously expensive
  - Avoid anything that is black or purple. These are colors of mourning.

INTERVIEW

- They may ask questions about income, religion and marital status

Business Culture in Germany

DRESS

- Dress in conservative, relatively plain business attire
  - Dark and conservative suits for men and women
  - Women should avoid excessively elaborate jewelry

BODY LANGUAGE / GESTURES

- Firm brief handshakes at arrival and departure

LANGUAGE / ADDRESSING OTHERS

- German is dominant language
  - May speak very good English but do not assume they do
- "Small talk" is not necessary
  - Not very relationship oriented
- Use last names to address the client
  - Use "Sie" then last name

HOW BUSINESS IS CONDUCTED

- Do not expect to be greeted by a stranger
  - Would prefer to be introduced by third party
- Be on time!
  - Even 5 minutes late is unacceptable
- Always make an appointment
- Make an appointment between 10:00am-1:00pm or 3:00pm and 5:00pm
- Do not schedule appointments on Friday afternoons
  - Some offices close by 2:00pm or 3:00pm
- Do not expect dinner or evening events
  - They enjoy taking time to themselves after business hours

CULTURALLY UNIQUE
- Germans will have six weeks of paid vacation
  - This means someone is always "in Urlaub" (on holiday)
  - Usually take vacations during July, August, December and Easter
- A gift is an important symbolic gesture
  - A small gift is polite
  - Never expected but appreciated except for social events
  - Flowers(not red roses) for the lady of the house is classic
  - Send a hand written thank you card to your hosts

RESUME
- Precise, detailed, accurate
- Will be compared to answers given in interview for consistency
- May cover point by point in interview

INTERVIEW
- Lengthy process – structured, systematic, trained interviewer
- Be prepared, know dates, responsibilities
- Consistency of answers with resume and repetitive questions
- Career needs to have been the result of accurate, careful planning, not haphazard or circumstantial. Job-hopping is not favorable.
- Describe accomplishments in facts, not boastfully
- Be serious, confident, assertive
- Personal questions are common
- Will be deemed worthy if background is consistent (resume, recommendations, answers)
- Multiple rounds of interviewing

Business Culture in Japan

DRESS
- Wear conservative suits
  - Pastel shirts are common
  - Take off your shoes in temples and homes
  - Women may wear slacks and heels

BODY LANGUAGE / GESTURES
- Quiet and low key manner
- A bow (ojigi) is a proper greeting
  - The depth of the bow depends on the rank or status
  - Bow lower if the persons status is higher than yours
- Will shake hands with Westerners but bow back to show respect
- The slightest gestures will be read into
- Avoid facial expressions and motioning
- The O.K. sign means money
- Pointing is rude
- It is not tolerable to spit, snort, sniffing and blowing your nose in public
- Laughter is looked at as embarrassment or distress
- Use direct eye contact

LANGUAGE / ADDRESSING OTHERS
- Japanese is dominant language
- Considered polite to frequently say "I'm sorry"
- When answering questions try not to use the word "No".
  - They would prefer " Yes, the document is not available"
- Hello should be said "Konnichiwa"
- Avoid topics like history and wars
- Use Mr. or Ms. Sometimes adding "San" to their last name

HOW BUSINESS IS CONDUCTED
- Make an appointment through direct contact or letter
- Being on time is very important
  - Being late is rude
- A working week is 48 hours without overtime pay
- Office hours are 9:00am to 5/5:30pm
- Avoid scheduling appointments December 28 to January 3, April 29 to May 5
  - These are holidays where many Japanese visit graves of their ancestors
- Refrain from discussing business with in the first few minutes of conversation

CULTURALLY UNIQUE
- Gift giving is very important
  - July 15 and January 1 gifts are exchanged among colleagues
  - Bring an assortment of gifts for your trip
  - A wrapped gift should be carried around in a bag so they do not know they are about to receive a gift
  - Paper colors are safest in pastel without bows.
  - Bring flowers or candy if invited to a home
  - Give your gift in private

RESUME
- Interviewer will go through thoroughly
- Keep factual, avoid showcasing outstanding background

INTERVIEW
- May be asked personal questions
- Multi-staged and group process
- Background checks are standard
- Lots of personal questions as business relationships are primary
- Serious process
- Answer factually, no bragging
- Demonstrate sincerity, warmth and willingness to work hard
- Character is more important than experience, they will be judgmental
- Repetitive questions, avoid impatience
- Frequent job change is not impressive, they are impressed by persistence
- Establish rapport with interviewer, common interests and topics
- Be prepared! Know company, culture and people

Business Culture in China

DRESS
- Conservative suits and ties
  - Bright colors are inappropriate
  - Women should wear suits or dresses with a high neck line
  - Flat shoes and low footwear

BODY LANGUAGE / GESTURES
- Will nod as a greeting; wait for them to initiate handshake
- Applause is a sign of welcome and you should applaud back
- Avoid facial expressions and gesture
- Do not use your hands when speaking. It annoys them.
- Use your whole hand to point rather than your index finger
- They dislike being touched by strangers
- Smiling is not noticeable
- Keep your hands away from your mouth. It is looked at as vulgar.
- You are subject to a heavy fine if found spitting in public

LANGUAGE / ADDRESSING OTHERS
- Chinese and Mandarin are dominant languages
- Acknowledge the most senior person in a group first
- Saying "no", "maybe" or "ill think about it" is considered impolite
- Make an initiative to use or learn some Chinese words
- "Small talk" is important
- Each person's name, in this order, has a family, generational, and first name.
- Should address with a title and their last name
  - Married women usually keep their maiden name

HOW BUSINESS IS CONDUCTED
- Being late for an appointment is a serious insult
- Schedule appointments April to June or September to October
- Business hours are 8:am-5:00pm Monday through Saturday
- They generally take a break between 12:00pm – 2:00pm
  - Almost everything shuts down between these hours

CULTURAL UNIQUENESS
- Express enthusiasm about the food you are eating
- Lavish gift giving was important, today the culture forbids lavish gift giving
  - They consider it to be bribery
- If you wish to give a gift do it privately in the context of friendship
- They will decline a gift three times before finally accepting so they will not appear greedy

- Pink, gold and silver are acceptable colors to wrap gifts
  - Wrapping in yellow paper with black writing is a gift given only to the dead
  - All the colors mean something different

INTERVIEW
- May be asked personal questions like age, income and marital status.

Business Culture in South Africa

DRESS
- Conservative suits are best. Short sleeves are okay as well but long sleeves are preferred

BODY LANGUAGE / GESTURES
- A very macho society so a firm handshake is important to make a good impression
- Maintain eye contact
- Its impolite to point at someone with your index finger wagging
- Talking with your hands in your pockets is rude
- African men will walk through a door way before women
- The "peace sign" (with your middle and index finger) when your palm is facing inward is the same as giving someone the finger
- Should speak in quiet voices
    - Talking about a common sport is okay
- Nod in agreement to show that you are listening
- They are physical when talking. Expect hand holding as a sign of friendship

LANGUAGE / ADDRESSING OTHERS
- Most are bilingual speaking English and Afrikaans
- Introductions are presented in order of seniority
- Some black South Africans will speak their native language even though they can speak English
- Never interrupt. It's rude.
- Address someone by using initials for their surname and then hyphenated last name
    - Example: K.R. Thorton-Rutherford

HOW BUSINESS IS CONDUCTED
- Schedule appointments as far in advance as possible
- Business is about friends and colleagues so they may be hesitant to be with you if they have never met you before
    - They would rather do mediocre business with a friend than excellent business with a stranger
- Expect to be kept waiting for 5 to 10 minutes
- Last minute cancellations are common
- You may have an appointment for 11:00am and the others will not show up until 3:00pm
    - You will never know unless you ask

CULTURALLY UNIQUE
- Never show impatience
- A small gift is greatly appreciated
    - Personalized and thoughtful gifts are appreciated
- When going to a dinner party always bring a gift like flowers or chocolates

INTERVIEW
- After a few conversations they make get personal and ask personal questions

JUNIOR COURSE

Week #12: Presentations about Information Interview/ Course Evaluation

NOTES

INFORMATIONAL INTERVIEW GRADING RUBRIC

Your name: _____

Person interviewed: _____

Title/company: _____

Date of interview: _____ Location of interview: _____

Presentation/Paper Expectations

TOPIC	VALUE – POINTS	POINTS EARNED	COMMENTS
PRESENTATION			
Introduction – yourself, state who was interviewed, their title, company, where and they were interviewed	5		
Their job responsibilities/ what you learned	15		
Reasons why this person was chosen, how their position/experience ties to your career plans	10		
What "words of wisdom" you learned	10		
Summary	5		
Presentation style – clear, articulate, 5 minutes	5		
PAPER – 2 PAGES			
Introduction – state who was interviewed, their title, company, where and they were interviewed	10		
Their job responsibilities/ what you learned	15		
Reasons why this person was chosen, how their position/experience ties to your career plans	10		
What "words of wisdom" you learned	10		
Summary	5		
TOTAL	100		

JUNIOR COURSE

Course Evaluation

NOTES

JUNIOR COURSE EVALUATION

Name (OPTIONAL) _____ Section #_____

In order to provide the best Professional Development Seminar program possible, we need your opinion of this course. All answers are confidential and only averages will be presented. Please provide your honest opinions.

► **DEMOGRAPHIC INFORMATION:**

1. Sex: ☐ Male   Female   ☐   **2. College Major:** _____

3. Year in College: 1ˢᵗ ☐,   2ⁿᵈ ☐,   3ʳᵈ ☐,   4ᵗʰ ☐,   other ☐

4. Would you be willing to return next year and describe this course to next year's class?
NO ☐   YES ☐
*If you answered yes, please let your instructor know.

► **YOUR OPINIONS OF THIS COURSE:**

1. In your opinion, what was the **best** thing or the most valuable experience about this course?

2. The **worst**?

3. If you were to return to next year's class, what advice would you offer those students?

► **YOUR OPINION OF THE CONTENT OF THIS COURSE:**

Instructions: please check the box on the right that corresponds to your opinion of each question below from strongly disagree, no opinion, agree and strongly agree.

♦ *This course helped me to…*	SD	D	N	A	SA
1. Gain a better understanding of my goals, and how college can help achieve them					
2. Understand how I am responsible for my college experience and making plans to guarantee my college success.					

► **SELF EVALUATION:**

The amount of work I did for this course was…

|-------☐----------------☐---------------☐---------------☐------------☐-------|
Quite A lot   Average   Very little

I am now aware that the time I spent was…

|-------☐----------------☐---------------☐---------------☐------------☐-------|
More than enough   Just right   Not nearly

The quality of my work for this course was…

|-------☐----------------☐---------------☐---------------☐------------☐-------|
Excellent   Above avg.   Average   Below avg.   Poor

I learned…

|-------☐----------------☐---------------☐---------------☐------------☐-------|
Very Much   Very little

►   **YOUR EVALUATION OF DIFFERENT PARTS OF THIS COURSE:**

INSTRUCTIONS: Please express your opinion of each question by placing a mark between each word.
For example:

♦   *The course syllabus was...*

Clear...	____|___|_x_|___|___|___|___	Vague
Casual...	____|___|___|___|___|_x_|___	Professional
Superficial...	____|___|_x_|___|___|___|___	Complete

♦ **My General opinion of the course is...**

Valuable	____|___|___|___|___|___|___	Useless
Challenging	____|___|___|___|___|___|___	Easy
Frustrating	____|___|___|___|___|___|___	Enjoyable
Boring	____|___|___|___|___|___|___	Interesting

♦ **In my opinion, the course assignments are...**

Valuable	____|___|___|___|___|___|___	Useless
Challenging	____|___|___|___|___|___|___	Easy
Frustrating	____|___|___|___|___|___|___	Enjoyable
Boring	____|___|___|___|___|___|___	Interesting

♦ **In my opinion, the time spent in class was...**

Valuable	____|___|___|___|___|___|___	Useless
Challenging	____|___|___|___|___|___|___	Easy
Frustrating	____|___|___|___|___|___|___	Enjoyable
Boring	____|___|___|___|___|___|___	Interesting

►   **YOUR EVALUATION OF THE INDIVIDUAL COURSE ASSIGNMENTS:**
    How <u>valuable</u> or <u>important</u> do you feel each topic covered this semester is?

Instructions: Please rate each of the following topics
          1 = "not valuable" to **3 = "no opinion or neutral"** to **5 = "very valuable"**
by marking the corresponding box to the right of each topic

♦ I would rate the value of the following topics as...	1	2	3	4	5
a.) Portfolio Contents for Junior Course…………………............					
b.) Resumes – electronic and paper……………………………...					
c.) Interviewing Skills: Professional Presentation/Communication Skills, Intro to Interviewing & Interviewing in Depth………………					
d.) Participation in Career Fair……………………………………...					
e.) Mock Interview as Interviewer………………………………….					
Mock Interview as Interviewee………………………………….					
Mock Interviews – overall………………………………….					
f.) Portfolio Sessions………………………………………………….					
g.) Career Search……………………………………………………..					
h.) Post Graduation Options………………………………………...					
i.) Junior Course Overall…………………………………………….					

JUNIOR FACULTY/INSTRUCTOR EVALUATION

Faculty/Instructor Name:_____

EVALUATION OF THE FACULTY/INSTRUCTOR:

The Course Faculty/Instructor...

	Strongly Disagree	Disagree	Neutral/ No opinion	Agree	Strongly agree
1. Was prepared and organized	☐	☐	☐	☐	☐
2. Was knowledgeable	☐	☐	☐	☐	☐
3. Expressed ideas clearly	☐	☐	☐	☐	☐
4. Encouraged class participation	☐	☐	☐	☐	☐
5. Demonstrated respect for the students	☐	☐	☐	☐	☐
6. Was enthusiastic	☐	☐	☐	☐	☐
7. Answered questions clearly & logically	☐	☐	☐	☐	☐
8. Used class time appropriately	☐	☐	☐	☐	☐
9. Was available outside of class	☐	☐	☐	☐	☐

Comments:

SENIOR COURSE

Week #1: Course Preview/Portfolios/ Senior Project

NOTES

COURSE SYLLABUS – SENIOR YEAR PDS

Faculty/Instructor: Office Hours:
Telephone: Office Location:
E-mail:

Course Purpose: "Initiating Career Plans and Developing Transition Skills"

Course Objective:
To provide the college senior with experiential education in the job search arena by offering information and direct contact with alumni and corporate recruiters. Students further enhance their portfolio within ethical and professional standards, with a focus on their intended career path.

Course Description:
The Senior course is designed to assist the senior in beginning the career search process, to provide the opportunity to solidify interview skills, to further develop an individual presentation through the portfolio, to gain knowledge regarding options available after graduation and how to identify and accept the emotions and issues regarding transitioning out of college. The heart of the course is the continued development of the student portfolio, a collection of each student's work, goals, experiences, accomplishments and achievements. Students will expand the portfolio with an emphasis on their individual achievement and success within their major. Another focus of the course is participation in the Senior Project, a project designed for each senior to leave their "legacy" to the incoming freshmen class or to further develop their skills and contacts in the recruitment process. Additionally, the class includes other relevant career topics as financial planning, recruiting, post-graduate options, and business etiquette.

Term of Course: Class will meet once a week for the first four weeks of the semester, followed by 4 weeks of workshops and programs (each senior must attend four), and then 4 weeks of class, for a total of 12 weeks.

Required Course Text/workbook: *The Professional Development Seminar: Junior and Senior Course.* Developed by Nichols College Professional Development Staff and Faculty. Second Edition. (2009). Kendall/Hunt Publishing Company.

Required Materials for Portfolio: Additional plastic sheet protectors.

Course Outline:

Date:

    Week #1:   **Introduction** - Overview of course. Review Senior syllabus.
                         Review of Student-Choice programs. Value/Contents of the Portfolio.
                         Resume Review. Introduction of the Senior Group Project. Begin
                         discussion about leaving college.
                         Assignment for week 2:
                         Update resume. Does not have to be turned in on resume paper.

Week #2: **Recruiting** – Present options available through Career Services (on-campus, off-campus, Career Fair), recruiting tips. Discuss various search methods, networking, and creation of an individual recruiting plan.
Assignment for week #3:
Register on "Road to Success"
Bring portfolio to next class.

Week #3: **Using the Portfolio in an Interview** – The value of a portfolio. How to use the portfolio in an interview. Practice using the portfolio with partners.

Week #4: **Money** - Current salary ranges. What are you worth on graduation day? Average cost of living expenses (rent, car payment, insurance, taxes, loan payments, etc.). Budget planning.
Assignment for Week #8:

Last Day to Withdraw from PDS

Weeks #5-7 **Student-Choice Programs** – Seniors must attend 4 programs – see registration form.

Week #8: **Assessments** – Understanding self and an introduction to the Personal Recruiting job Search Plan assignment.

Week #9: **Business Etiquette, Ethics, and Networking** – Professional behavior, writing, manners, proper introductions, etc. Developing professional connections and networking.
Assignment due week # 10:
Finish preparation for Senior Group Project presentation, and one page handout.

Week #10: **Presentations – Senior Group Project**

Week #11: **Presentations – Senior Group Project**
Assignment due week #12:
Complete Personal Recruiting/Job Search Plan
Complete portfolio

Week #12: **Affective/Transition Issues, First Year on the Job** - Discussion about leaving - how to say goodbye, develop strategies for leaving, where to live after graduation, etc. What the job environment is like, how to adapt.
PORTFOLIOS DUE AT CLASS

Grading: Final Grades will be composed of the following elements:

Resume	10%
Attendance at the Student-Choice Programs	20%
Senior Group Project	15%
Personal Recruiting/Job Search Plan	15%
Portfolio	30%
Class Participation	10%
	100%

Absence Policy:

This course is a graduation requirement. Only one absence is permitted. The final grade will be one letter grade lower for each additional absence. Students must attend the course section they are scheduled for.

Student Agreement:

You are willing to complete the requirements as given in the syllabus and discussed in class to earn a grade for the course. The College reserves the right to alter or change the assignments and/or requirements to better meet student needs as deemed necessary.

Academic Honesty Policy:

Enrollment in an academic course at Nichols College obligates the student to follow the College's Academic Honesty Policy, the violation of which can lead to serious disciplinary action. The Policy may be stated simply as follows:

> *The College expects all academic work submitted by a student (papers, exams, projects, computer programs, etc.) to be the student's own. Plagiarism (as defined below), cheating during examinations, and assisting others in the acts of plagiarism or cheating, are expressly prohibited by the Policy. In sum, a student's academic performance must be an honest representation of the student's ability.*

The following are detailed descriptions of some possible Academic Honesty Policy violations:

1. Plagiarism is defined as the unaccredited use of words or ideas, which are the result of other persons' creative efforts.

   Examples of plagiarism include the following:

   A. Copying of other persons' work during examinations, with or without their permission.

   B. Duplication of other persons' homework, themes, essays, reports, research papers, computer code, spreadsheets, graphics, etc. with or without their permission.

   C. Use of specific passages or detailed use of specific ideas as set forth in books, journals, magazines, etc. without proper citation (footnotes, bibliography).

   D. Use of materials provided by term paper services.

2. Complicity in plagiarism by condoning copying of one's own work including homework, themes, essays, reports, research papers, computer code, spreadsheets, graphics, etc.

3. Use of notes or "crib sheets" during examinations (unless the instructor specifically authorizes use of such materials or an "open book" examination format).

   Examples of penalties imposed for violation of the Honesty Policy include failing grades, forced withdrawal from courses or suspension from the College. The instructor normally resolves cases but in some instances a student may be subjected to a formal hearing conducted by a committee of the faculty. The severity of the penalties suggests that it is most important for all Nichols students to fully understand the specific kinds of behavior that violate the Policy.

Nichols College Guidelines for College-Sponsored Activities:
Participation in extracurricular activities such as academic field trips, cultural experiences, and intercollegiate athletics is viewed as an integral part of the total student experience at Nichols College. Faculty members are encouraged to provide students, in good academic standing, the accommodations necessary to fulfill their extracurricular/athletic commitments. For student-athletes, the commitments include competition and travel schedules as well as those areas critical to the "game experiences", i.e. necessary safety precautions such as visiting the athletic training staff prior to competition and adequate warm-up prior to competition.

An excused absence does NOT excuse students from completing coursework missed during their absence. Prior to missing class, students are expected to notify their instructors and provide them with information regarding the departure date/time and discuss how missed work will be made up.

SENIOR GROUP PROJECT/PRESENTATION

Assignment due Week 10 or 11

Goal:
The Senior Group Project is designed to:
1) provide the opportunity for students to research various tools available to assist with conducting industry research and the job search, and
2) teach other students how to access and utilize these resources.

Activity:
Each group will research a specific topic and present their findings in class through:
1) an interactive group presentation to the class (20 minutes). This presentation will teach others how to access and utilize the resources and must include an activity with class participation; and
2) a one page summary of the findings to distribute to classmates and the instructor.

Process:
Groups will consist of 2-4 students. Each group will explore one of the following aspects of the job search process:

Job Search by Industry or by Major
Research the methods and tools to find positions within a specific industry or based on a major. What are the industry-specific resources that exist? How are these accessed? How valuable are they? What are the recruiting methods specific to the major or industry? What resources do people in the field recommend? You may want to conduct informational interviews of people in the field. Include resources such as: websites, professional organizations, and networking opportunities.

Group #1: Industry: _____
      Student names: _____

_____

Group #2: Industry: _____
      Student names: _____

_____

Vault
Go to the Vault webpage and explore the numerous ways this site can be used in a job search. What is Vault? What does the site contain? What are the benefits of using this site? Become a "mini expert" with the site. Demonstrate some of the best aspects of the site for a job search (access Vault through Career Services webpage: www.vault.com).

Group #3: Vault Online Library
      Student names: _____

_____

Networking

What is networking? How is it best accomplished? What percentage of people find their job through networking? What opportunities are there to network professionally with others – online, events, professional organizations? Incorporate a role play or demonstration of meeting and communicating with someone for networking purposes.

Group #4: Networking:
    Student names: _____

_____

Job Search Resources

A. Research online search engines and employment sites. What are the best sites? Why? Which are targeted sites? Which are general sites? What is the difference? Which sites would you recommend? Why? Which are the most popular sites? Consider monster.com, monstertrak.com, careerbuilder.com, yahoojobs.com, and others.
What is the Occupational Outlook Handbook? How can it be used in a job search? (online at http://www.bls.gov/OCO/ and in book form in the Career Services and PDS offices).

Group #5: Online Resources:
    Student names: _____

_____

B. Community and non-profit groups, professional organizations, and directories offer invaluable information in a job search. Explore the various organizations which have unique resources to offer including: Chambers of Commerce, United Way and other non-profits, Yellowpages.com, and a super pages search. What are the best resources? How are these resources best used? How can these be helpful for a country-wide or international search?

Group #6: Organizations/Directories:
    Student names: _____

_____

Research Process:

Students may utilize any resource deemed appropriate to collect information on the topic, including: websites, books in the Career Services Library, books in the Nichols Library, online resources, periodicals, interviews, and more.

Summary Page:

Each group must complete a one page summary of their findings, including a list of resources, and distribute one to each student in the class and a copy to the course instructor. Copies of the handout may be made in the Academic Affairs Office in Conant Hall.

Presentation:

A 20 minute group presentation to the class to include:
1) A presentation demonstrating how to use the resources selected, with all group members presenting. This should be a teaching presentation – teaching others how to use this resource.
2) An interactive activity with all students in the class participating.

Topics to Address:

The presentation and one page summary should cover the following:
1) What is the resource – definition, characteristics
2) When to use this resource – in which situation(s) is it best?
3) How to access this resource?
4) Why use this resource?
5) Who uses this resource – specific group of people? Percentage of job seekers who find jobs using this resource?
6) Strengths of this resource.
7) Limitations of this resource.
8) List of suggested resources – websites, books, periodicals, etc.
9) Other topics deemed appropriate.

Multi-media:

Groups may use whatever media they choose to present their findings – PowerPoint, demonstration of websites, video, posters, handouts, brochures, etc.

Grading:

The grade will be a group grade (individuals within the group receive the same grade). This grade represents 15% of each student's final course grade. The grade will be based on the following:
1) Quality of project (well organized presentation, clear multi-media items, utilized best resources on the topic, ability to define and explain topic)
2) Quantity/variety (a reasonable amount of resources presented, variety of resources used)
3) Delivery (clarity of presentation, ability to explain/define terms, flow of delivery)
4) Professionalism (use of professional language, business dress, professional quality of multi-media items)
5) Effort (well prepared, resources readily available, ability to demonstrate what was learned on the topic)

SENIOR GROUP PROJECT/PRESENTATION GRADING RUBRIC

Group Member Names: _____

_____

Date of Presentation: _____

TOPIC	VALUE – POINTS	POINTS EARNED	COMMENTS
Introduction – group members, state topic and its value in the job search	5		
Comprehensive presentation, including major highlights	30		
Strengths/weaknesses of using this in a search	10		
Why this should be part of a job search	10		
Engagement of students – use of media, activity, or classroom discussion	10		
Summary, wrap-up	5		
One page summary of highlights/ recommendations	20		
Group membership – equality of work and presentation	10		
TOTAL	100		

PERSONAL RECRUITING/JOB SEARCH PLAN

Assignment due Week 12

Overview: There are **four parts** of the Personal Recruiting/Job Search Plan:
1) Job Search Intentions: 2-3 paragraphs of your intended job search plans **(10%)**
2) Updating and critiquing of resumes, cover letter, and reference list **(20%)**
3) Complete any 4 of the 7 parts of the Job Search Resources section: **(60%)**
     a) Company websites
     b) Major Job Search engines
     c) On/Off Campus Recruiting in Career Services
     d) Sunday newspaper "Help Wanted" search
     e) Networking Opportunities
     f) Recruitment Agencies
     g) Career Fairs
4. Summary: 2-3 paragraphs of the next steps of your job search **(10%)**

Be sure to fully complete all four parts. These components are explained in greater detail in this handout. <u>This assignment must be typed.</u>

Preparation: Before you embark on your job search, you need to determine what type(s) of positions you will apply for and at what type(s) of organization(s). There are several things to consider: What do you enjoy? What are you qualified for? What industries will you enjoy working in? Do you prefer small, medium or large organizations? Will you search for a position in a public or private organization or a government /agency? Use the resources/tools you've learned about in Junior and Senior PDS to explore your options. A strategic job search plan makes for a productive and efficient search!

PART 1: JOB SEARCH INTENTIONS: Write 2-3 paragraphs reflecting on what type of job(s)/position(s) you will focus on for this recruiting plan. Include the geographic location(s) of interest as well as types of companies/organizations or company names. Attach *typewritten* pages.

PART 2: UPDATE MATERIALS: Before you begin your job search you'll need to have the items listed below updated and critiqued by a trusted source (career counselor, PDS instructor, family or friend who works in college recruiting, etc.) Fill in the information below & attach the critiqued materials:

	Date Updated	Critique Date	Person's Name/Position
Resume			
Cover Letter			
Eresume (Text Resume) (Optional for Extra Credit)			
List of References			

PART 3: JOB SEARCH RESOURCES: Complete 4 of the following 7 resources in the job search.

□ **RESOURCE 1: <u>COMPANY WEBSITES</u>**
1) Locate the websites of at least 3 companies you are interested in. List these sites and indicate current openings that you may qualify for:

2) Complete an online application at one of these company websites for a position you are interested in. Print the completed application and then submit it online to the company. Include the printed application for this project.

a) www._____

    List job titles and application deadlines for open positions you qualify for: _____
_____
_____

b) www._____

    List job titles and application deadlines for open positions you qualify for: _____
_____
_____

c) www._____

    List job titles and application deadlines for open positions you qualify for: _____
_____
_____

□ **RESOURCE 2: <u>MAJOR JOB SEARCH ENGINES</u>** (such as www.monster.com, www.careerbuilder.com)
1) Locate the websites of at least 3 job search engines you are interested in. List these sites & indicate 3 current openings that you may qualify for from each site:
a) www._____

    List 3 job titles and application deadlines for open positions you qualify for: _____
_____
_____

b) www._____

    List 3 job titles and application deadlines for open positions you qualify for: _____
_____
_____

c) www._____

    List 3 job titles and application deadlines for open positions you qualify for: _____
_____
_____

2) What pros and cons have you found while searching and applying for jobs on major job search engines? Be specific._____
_____
_____

□ **RESOURCE 3: <u>ON-CAMPUS RECRUITING PROGRAM IN THE OFFICE OF CAREER SERVICES</u>**
(Recruiting Schedule is posted on Road to Success)

1) List 3 companies/positions you are interested in from the On-Campus Recruiting List:

a) _____
b) _____
c) _____

2) Complete the Preference Sheet and submit it along with copies of your resume to Career Services to apply for at least one available position. Place an asterisk (*) next to the company above that you are applying to.

3) Did you get accepted for this interview? If yes, what will do you to prepare? If no, what can you do differently to increase your chances of being accepted for similar interviews?

□ **RESOURCE 4: <u>SUNDAY NEWSPAPER "HELP WANTED" SECTIONS</u>**
1) List newspapers and edition dates of those that you have read the Help Wanted section.
a) _____
b) _____
c) _____

2) Clip and attach at least two job advertisements for positions you will apply for from these newspapers.

□ **RESOURCE 5: <u>NETWORKING OPPORTUNITIES</u>** List 10 people who you could network with. Write 2-3 paragraphs on how networking will help you in your job search.

Top People in My Network (Name up to 10)	Relationship	Recent Contact? Date/Details	Action Items/Follow-up Notes (include how you plan to communicate with this person in the near future)
1.			
2.			
3.			
4.			
5.			
6.			
7.			
8.			
9.			
10.			

□ RESOURCE 6: <u>RECRUITMENT AGENCIES – THIRD PARTY STAFFING AGENCIES</u>

There are pros and cons to utilizing staffing agencies. You should do your research before you decide whether to apply for jobs via third party agencies. Should you choose to utilize agencies we recommend that you use no more than two at a time during your entry level job search.

1) Agency Name:	
Website:	
Recruiter's Name: (attach business card)	
What industries do they specialize in?	

2) Agency Name:	
Website:	
Recruiter's Name: (attach business card)	
What industries do they specialize in?	

3) In 2-3 paragraphs, explain how you think you will benefit from the relationship you have established with these staffing agencies.

□ RESOURCE 7: <u>CAREER FAIRS</u> – Choose 3 upcoming Career Fairs (or Virtual Career Fairs) in your area and complete the following:

Name of Career Fair/Sponsoring Organization	City/State/Website/ Location of Career Fair	Top Companies of Interest to You	Jobs Being Offered by Each Top Company of Interest
1.			
2.			
3.			

4) PART 4: SUMMARY Write 2-3 paragraphs stating how you feel about your job search. Things to consider: Are you confident that you have developed a plan that will aid you in successfully landing a good entry-level job? What have you learned? Where are you headed? What other resources will you consider utilizing? Do you feel confident, overwhelmed, stressed, excited, etc.? What are your next steps? Attach *typewritten* pages.

GRADUATE SCHOOL ASSSIGNMENT FORM

(may be completed in lieu of Personal Recruiting/Job Search Plan)

Assignment due Week 12

1. Complete the following for 3 graduate programs/schools of interest.
2. Provide citations for your information.

Name of College/University: _____

Name of program/department you are applying to: _____

Name of the degree you are applying for:_____

1) How will this degree help you meet your future goals? What do you intend to do with this degree upon graduation:_____

_____

_____

2) What is the reputation of this program?

_____

_____

3) How accessible is the faculty? What is the student to faculty ratio?

_____

_____

4) How much are the yearly tuition and fees? What are your plans for affording this program?

_____

_____

5) What kind of career services does the program offer? What are the placement rates for recent graduates?

_____

_____

6) What are the university facilities like? (library, computers, offices/labs/studios, etc.).

_____

_____

7) Do you like the city/setting of the college? Why/why not?

_____

_____

8) How is the cost of living? Where will you live?

_____

_____

9) How long will it take to complete this degree?

_____

10) What kind of connections can you make with alumni? Does the school have facilitated ways to get you in touch with alumni?

_____

_____

_____

Name of College/University: _____

Name of program/department you are applying to: _____

Name of the degree you are applying for:_____

1) How will this degree help you meet your future goals? What do you intend to do with this degree upon graduation:_____
_____
_____

2) What is the reputation of this program?
_____
_____

3) How accessible is the faculty? What is the student to faculty ratio?
_____
_____

4) How much are the yearly tuition and fees? What are your plans for affording this program?
_____
_____

5) What kind of career services does the program offer? What are the placement rates for recent graduates?
_____
_____

6) What are the university facilities like? (library, computers, offices/labs/studios, etc.).
_____
_____

7) Do you like the city/setting of the college? Why/why not?
_____
_____

8) How is the cost of living? Where will you live?
_____
_____

9) How long will it take to complete this degree?
_____

10) What kind of connections can you make with alumni? Does the school have facilitated ways to get you in touch with alumni?
_____
_____
_____

Name of College/University: _____

Name of program/department you are applying to: _____

Name of the degree you are applying for:_____

1) How will this degree help you meet your future goals? What do you intend to do with this degree upon graduation:_____
_____
_____

2) What is the reputation of this program?
_____
_____

3) How accessible is the faculty? What is the student to faculty ratio?
_____
_____

4) How much are the yearly tuition and fees? What are your plans for affording this program?
_____
_____

5) What kind of career services does the program offer? What are the placement rates for recent graduates?
_____
_____

6) What are the university facilities like? (library, computers, offices/labs/studios, etc.).
_____
_____

7) Do you like the city/setting of the college? Why/why not?
_____
_____

8) How is the cost of living? Where will you live?
_____
_____

9) How long will it take to complete this degree?
_____

10) What kind of connections can you make with alumni? Does the school have facilitated ways to get you in touch with alumni?
_____
_____
_____

SENIOR YEAR INFORMATION SHEET

Name: Home Phone: Major:

College Email: Personal Email:

1. Career Goals: (Be as specific as possible at this point – field/industry, position(s), companies, etc.)

2. How do you intend to find a job before graduation?

3. Have you completed an internship? If so, where, and what was your title? Do you plan to complete one (or another) before graduation?

4. List topics that you are interested in learning about in Senior PDS and/or things you would like to cover this semester:

5. List topics or aspects about Senior PDS that you are not particularly interested in:

6. What are your goals for Senior PDS?

7. Who was your Junior PDS Faculty/Instructor?

SENIOR COURSE

Week # 2: Recruiting

NOTES

ON-CAMPUS RECRUITING

WHAT IS ON-CAMPUS RECRUITING?

Company recruiters interview students in the Office of Career Services (OCS) on a given day. Feedback from the interview is available from the Recruitment Coordinator following the interview. OCS has launched a recruiting program, *Road to Success*. Created with you in mind, this site provides participating students with the ability to:

- Maintain an online Personal Calendar

- Manage multiple resumes, cover letters, and other employment related documents

- Search for and apply for job opportunities online

- Schedule on-campus interviews

- View and RSVP for career events

- Much more!

Please log on to *Road to Success* to update and/or create your account and begin using the system. If you experience any problems or have questions, please contact Career Services at 508-213-2489 or email **careerservices@nichols.edu**.

Your default login is:

firstname.lastname

Your default password is:

your birth date, for example: 3/5/1989

NOTES

SENIOR COURSE

Week # 3: Using the Portfolio in an Interview

NOTES

EFFECTIVELY USING THE PORTFOLIO IN AN INTERVIEW

Once you have fully prepared for the interview, you can begin planning how you will use the portfolio in the interview. Of course, all well-intentioned plans are subject to change once the interview begins, since the interviewer is in charge. However, some planning and overriding goals will help you to be more effective using the portfolio in the interview.

How to Prepare the Portfolio for the Interview

Your portfolio will include a variety of items, demonstrating the various skills you possess. As a Nichols student, your portfolio will include items from each of the following categories:

- Career and Professional Planning/Growth
- Teamwork/Leadership Skills
- Communication Skills
- Analytical/Problem Solving/Critical Thinking Skills
- Technology Related Skills
- Optional Category

Additional items to be included are: portfolio cover with name, table of contents, introductory statement, resume and letter of reference.

The above categories are based on <u>The Top Ten Qualities Employers Seek</u>, an annual survey by the National Association of Colleges and Employers. Knowing the qualities employers embrace allows you to build your portfolio to display skills relative to today's job market.

By including these various items you will be demonstrating a broad range of skills and experiences that will be impressive to most any interviewer. It is important that each of the items has a brief description about what the item is, when it was created, why you included it and what you have learned from creating this item or the experience you gained. Additionally, your portfolio will need to be neat, organized and look professional.

There are many ways to set up the portfolio for an interview. You may want to keep the entire contents intact to show a broad scope of skills and experiences or you may want to focus the portfolio on more specific areas relevant to a particular position. The Nichols portfolio is a 3-ring binder with each item enclosed in a plastic sheet protector, and therefore, changing the order and contents of a portfolio is easy.

There are several ways to prepare the portfolio. The benefits of each of these methods will depend on the interview, the interviewer and your personal preference.

Type of Portfolio	Items in Portfolio	Benefits	Drawbacks
General Portfolio	All original items	Every item is available if needed, demonstrates broad skills	A lot of information to organize & locate
Specific Portfolio	Only items relevant to position applying for	Focus on specific qualities	Doesn't demonstrate broader skills
Combination Portfolio	All original items, but relevant items placed first in the portfolio	Specific items easy to access, items given importance	Method of organization may be confusing

When in doubt as to how to organize the portfolio, prepare a general portfolio. You will have every item at your disposal. An interview can take an unexpected turn and with a general portfolio the entire contents will always be accessible.

It is essential that you become familiar with your portfolio and know where each item is located. You will look organized and prepared if you can find an item as you need it. This preparation will allow the portfolio to complement you in the interview and not become a distraction.

How to Carry the Portfolio to the Interview

The portfolio may be carried alone to the interview or it may be placed in a professional-looking briefcase. Either way, try to keep it as inconspicuous as possible until you need it. If you choose to carry it, be sure to carry it with your left arm since your right arm will need to be free to shake the interviewer's hand. By choosing to use a briefcase, you will also have the option of including a pad, pen and business cards inside. If the portfolio is in a briefcase, you will want to bring it out once you settle in for the interview. Set it aside and keep the focus on you, the interviewee.

Possession of the Portfolio

When entering the interview, if the interviewer asks what the portfolio is, the best response is to reply, "I have brought my portfolio with me. This portfolio includes examples of my best work and demonstrates the various skills I have. I will ask you later if I may use it to show my work as it relates to the questions you may ask." Hopefully this response will send a message to the interviewer, that while this is a valuable document, you are not quite ready to show it. The interviewer may or may not accept this answer.

Use of portfolios in the interview process is a new concept and most interviewers have not seen a portfolio. They may be curious about what it is and may want to see it right away. If the interviewer wants to see the portfolio, certainly don't disagree with him/her. Share the portfolio. The interviewer may choose to go through the portfolio page by page. While this process may not be the most effective way to use the portfolio, there is still some value in this, particularly if the interviewer is impressed with your portfolio. As often as possible, try to guide the interviewer to the most useful items. When you come to one of these items, make the most of the opportunity and describe the importance of the item and define the skills you have relative to the item.

The best method for using the portfolio is to use it periodically to support your answer to a question. Always answer the question fully and then ask if you may show an item in the portfolio to support your response. After showing the portfolio, try to casually pull the portfolio back into your possession and keep it until you are ready to use it again. The portfolio is best used periodically and not necessarily in response to every question. If you have planned ahead, you will know exactly which items you want the interviewer to see. Try to fit as many of these items into this process as possible.

Using the Portfolio

How you use the portfolio in an interview can make or break the impression the recruiter has of you. It is essential that you remain confident and professional in the manner you carry yourself at the interview. The most important aspect of using a portfolio in an interview is to remember that the portfolio serves to *support* you in the interview. It is not the focus of the interview. *You* are the focus of the interview.

First and foremost, you must build rapport with the recruiter. Try small talk in the beginning before the formal interview begins. Always smile and be positive. Your personality must come out and you need to "connect" on a human level with the recruiter. Be sure to be sincere with your answers, and always be honest.

Once the interview is successfully underway and you believe you have established rapport with the interviewer, you then may begin using the portfolio. When a question is asked that you could support by using the portfolio, first answer the question fully. This is important. You will want to be sure to demonstrate your communication skills by fully answering the question before using the portfolio. After you have answered, you can then ask the recruiter if he/she would like to see an item in your portfolio which supports your answer. If he/she says no, don't be offended just follow the interviewers lead to the next step in the interview.

However, if there is interest, then turn to the page you need and face the portfolio toward the recruiter so he/she may fully see your item. You will need to be familiar with the contents of your portfolio so that you may go right to that item. Be sure to explain the item – what it is, why you included it, what you learned from the process of completing the item, the skills you used in completing it and the skills you now possess. Obviously, you will want to take just a minute or so to explain the item so you may not be able to cover each of these topics. Address as many of these areas as you can while still allowing the interview to flow. Take the lead from the recruiter. If he/she asks a lot of questions, then continue to discuss the item. If, however, there is little or no interest, move on in the interview. The portfolio may be used multiple times during the interview, but again, remember that it is a supplement to you, so use it sparingly.

What if the interviewer shows no interest in the portfolio?

Use of a portfolio in an interview is a relatively new concept and most interviewers have never seen one before. This may spark interest or it may not. Most interviewers are very intrigued by a portfolio and impressed by the skills you are able to demonstrate in it. However, there are recruiters who will show no interest in a portfolio. There could be several reasons for this. First of all, they may not know what it is and therefore how effective it can be. Some interviewers stick to what they know and are uncomfortable with new ideas. Second, lack of response from an interviewer could be due to a time constraint. Many interviewers, especially those conducting a screening interview, may have a prescribed pattern in place and cannot sway from their planned itinerary. However, a hiring manager may be more interested in the portfolio since they usually are looking for more specific skills than a human resources generalist.

The Value of Your Portfolio

Your portfolio is very valuable! Developing a portfolio takes you through a very important self-assessment process and allows you to identify your assets. This process alone puts you several steps ahead of other candidates applying for the same position. Your portfolio will help you shine in the interview, whether it is actually used on not. However, with any luck, the interviewer will recognize the value of the portfolio and ask to see the contents. By planning how to use your portfolio in the interview, you will be prepared and stand out in the crowd. Take pride in your hard work, be confident in who you are, and enjoy the interview process!

Written by Dawn C. Sherman,
Director of the Professional Development Seminar Program
Nichols College

USING THE PORTFOLIO IN AN INTERVIEW –
QUESTIONS

Interviewer:
Ask your partner 10 of the questions below.

Interviewee:
Respond to each question with the 3 A's: *answer* the question, *ask* if you can show an example, *articulate*/explain an example from your portfolio which supports your answer. For the sake of this exercise, use your portfolio to support the answer to each question.

Switch roles.
Interviewer:
Ask the interviewee the remaining 10 questions.

1) Are you most productive working alone or in a group?
2) What skills do you offer that are most relevant to this job?
3) How do you stay current in the field?
4) What new skills or ideas do you bring to the job that other candidates aren't likely to offer?
5) What are some of your strongest skills?
6) What are your strengths?
7) How is your experience relevant to this job?
8) What skills do you think are most critical to this position? Give an example.
9) How good are your writing skills?
10) What computer systems and software do you know?
11) Give me an example of how you saw a project through, despite obstacles.
12) Share an example of your determination.
13) Describe a time when you tackled a tough or unpopular assignment.
14) Would your current boss describe you as the kind of employee who goes the extra mile?
15) Employees tend to be either concept oriented or task oriented. How do you describe yourself?
16) What would your colleagues tell me about your attention to detail?
17) Describe a professional skill you've developed in your most recent position.
18) What's the most creative or innovative project you've worked on?
19) Give me proof of your persuasiveness.
20) Describe an improvement you personally initiated.

NOTES

SENIOR COURSE

Week # 4: Money

NOTES

MIND OVER MONEY – FINANCIAL

WHAT WILL BE MINE ON GRADUATION DAY?

Cash (Currency and Checking)   _____

Savings   _____

Investments   _____
     Real Estate   _____
     Corporate Stock   _____
     Various Bonds   _____
     Mutual Funds   _____
     Real Estate   _____
     Automobiles   _____
     Furniture   _____
     Clothing   _____
     Collectibles   _____

Retirement Plans
     IRA/Keogh
     401 (K)
     403 B)   _____

Other Assets   _____

           Owned: _____

HOW MUCH WILL I OWE OTHERS ON GRADUATION DAY?

A. Student and other College-related Loans   _____
B. Automobile Loans   _____
C. Charge Cards   _____
D. Other Loans and Debts   _____

           Owed: _____

SO WHAT WILL I BE WORTH ON GRADUATION DAY?

(Subtract what you owe from what you own)   Total: _____

Created by Richard Lee Hilliard, Chartered Financial Consultant

THIS INFORMATION IS FOR YOUR USE ONLY AND WILL BE KEPT CONFIDENTIAL

- CONFIDENTIAL –

MIND OVER MONEY
STUDENT ESTIMATES – ANNUAL FIGURES

Compensation – Primary job $ _____
(avg. for Class of 2008 = $39,000)

Other income $ _____

TOTAL INCOME	$ _____

Taxes (deduct 40% of total above) $ _____
Federal, state, town (house/condo, auto/boat, dog license, sales tax, etc.)

Rent/Mortgage $ _____

Utilities (electric, telephone, gas, etc.) $ _____

Transportation: car payment, public transportation, $ _____
gas, repairs, parking, tolls
Ex.: new car costs: Volkswagen Beetle $22,000, Honda Accord $24,500,
Corvette $52,500, Porsche 911Turbo $145,000

Insurance (auto, medical, homeowner's, life) $ _____

Food (groceries, restaurants) $ _____

Furniture/Household (paper goods, linens, cleaning $ _____
supplies, dishes/pans, vacuum, rugs, curtains, etc.)

Student Loans $ _____

Clothing/shoes, dry cleaning $ _____

Personal items/hygiene products $ _____

Medical expenses (co-payments, glasses, etc.) $ _____

Electronics (computer/internet, TV/cable, cell phone) $ _____

Entertainment (movies, vacations, concert tickets, etc.) $ _____

Savings $ _____

Misc. $ _____

TOTAL EXPENSES	$ _____

NET	$ _____

Created by Richard Lee Hilliard, Chartered Financial Consultant

MIND OVER MONEY – AFFORDING THE LIFE I WANT

THE NICHOLS SENIOR MIND OVER MONEY REALITY CHECK

In the space below write a reality-based sentence briefly describing where you expect to be working and how much you think you will be earning when you graduate. Include graduate school or military earnings.

_____

_____

_____

_____

_____

_____

_____

THE SENIOR PROFESSIONAL DEVELOPMENT PRIORITY SURVEY*

The Nichols Business Manager has just handed you a cash refund of $200. Read each pair of words on the following list and circle the item or activity on which you prefer to spend the money. Select only one item and do not try to split the money or it will be taken back and you will never see it again!

Savings or Personal appearance	Social activities or Savings
Clothes or Social activities	Hobbies or Clothes
Sports or Eating out	Personal appearance or Sports
Eating out or Savings	Church/charity or Eating out
Paying a debt or Clothes	Savings or Paying a debt
Social activities or Church/charity	Clothes or Social activities
Hobbies or Paying a debt	Sports or Hobbies
Personal appearance or Sports	Eating out or Personal appearance
Church/charity or Hobbies	Paying a debt or Church/charity

Now count the number of times you circled each item or activity and list the totals below

____ Savings	____ Eating out	____ Hobbies
____ Clothes	____ Paying a debt	____ Personal appearance
____ Sports	____ Social activities	____ Church/charity

The above list, from the highest number to lowest number, will give you some idea where you are more likely to spend your money.

THIS INFORMATION IS FOR YOUR USE ONLY AND WILL BE KEPT CONFIDENTIAL

- CONFIDENTIAL -

MIND OVER MONEY – DESIRES AND NEEDS

The purpose of this exercise is to examine what is important in your life as you approach your Nichols College Graduation Day. To accomplish this you will need to separate things that would be nice to have from things you must have. For example, while it might be *nice* to have a new Corvette … you *must* have a place to live. You will also want to separate non-financial from financial goals. For example, being kind to your relatives might be a very worthy goal yet the actual dollar cost could be zero.

IN THE SPACE THAT FOLLOWS, BRIEFLY OUTLINE SOME OF YOUR MORE IMPORTANT LIFE GOALS AND PUT AN ASTERISK (*) NEXT TO THE ONES THAT ARE IMPORTANT _AND_ COST MONEY.

Created by Richard Lee Hilliard, Chartered Financial Consultant

MIND OVER MONEY – A TAXING PROBLEM

TAXES AND MAKING ENDS MEET!

None of the following taxes existed in 1906 and about half did not exist in 1956.

Accounts Receivable Tax
Alternative Minimum Tax
Bottle Return Tax
Building Permit Tax
Capital Gains Tax
Cigarette Tax
Corporate Income Tax
Court Fines (indirect tax)
Cat License Tax
Dog License Tax
Excise Tax
Federal Income Tax
Federal Unemployment Tax
Fishing License Tax
Food License Tax
Fuel Permit Tax
Gasoline Tax
Hunting License Tax
Inheritance Tax
Inheritance Interest Tax
Inventory Tax
IRS Penalty Tax
Liquor Tax
Local Income Tax
Luxury Tax
Marriage License Tax
Medicare Tax
Property Tax
Septic Permit Tax
Airline Taxes/Fees

Social Security Tax
Road Usage Taxes
Sales Tax
Recreational Vehicle Tax
Road Toll Booth Tax
School Tax
State Income Tax
State Unemployment Tax
Telephone Federal Excise Tax
Telephone Universal Service Tax
Telephone Surcharge Taxes
Telephone Recurring Charges Tax
Telephone State and Local Taxes
Telephone Recurring/Non Tax
Toll Bridge Taxes
Toll Tunnel Tax
Traffic Fines
Automobile Registration Taxes
Trailer Registration Tax
Utility Tax
Vehicle License Registration Tax
Vehicle Sales Tax
Watercraft Registration Tax
Watercraft Trailer Registration Tax
Watercraft State/Local Tax
Well Permit Tax
Workers' Compensation Tax
Real Estate Tax
Service Charge Tax

rlh 2006

THE BENEFITS & SALARY YOU DESERVE
Questions about Salary & Benefits

If the question of salary is brought up too early during the interview, try to redirect the discussion. You could say something like, "Before we discuss my salary requirements, could you tell me a little more about the position?" The more facts you have about the position, the better opportunity you will have to identify what it is worth.

If an employer asks you about your salary expectations, it is wise to verify your understanding of the position. For example, "Let's see if I completely understand the responsibilities..." You can finish your response with a question of your own: "What range did you have in mind for someone with my experience and skills?" If they don't answer, then give a range of what you think you are worth in the marketplace.

Know how a variety of salaries play out in reality. For instance, a job might offer you $200 more of discretionary income per month than another job of a lower salary, but would require you to spend $85 more per month on tolls and gasoline because of where the company is located. You might negotiate $7,000 more a year only to find out that it will bump you into a higher tax bracket. Try to think of all the various dollar amounts in advance because during negotiations you might not have time to think it through.

Lastly, know the entire compensation plan, not just what the annual income or hourly wage is. Consider year-end bonuses, commissions, signing bonuses, overtime policy, relocation expenses, and performance reviews.

Below is a list of benefits that may be offered by the company you choose to work for. Remember to always fully understand the benefit package prior to accepting a job.

Tuition Reimbursement	Vacations
Sick Leave	Employee Assistance Program
Retirement Savings and Profit Sharing Plans	Computer Loan Program
Flexible Spending Accounts	Referral Program
Research and Study Leave	Profit Sharing Plan
401K/ 403B Plan	Dental Plan Options
Medical Plan Options	Vision Service Plan
Short/ Long Term Disability Plan	Employee Life Insurance
Dependent Life Insurance	Domestic Partner Coverage
Holidays	

SALARY NEGOTIATIONS GUIDELINE

Tips for raising the subject of
compensation and negotiating salary

Understand the value of your degree and what you are worth based on your prior experience. Do your research!

Ask your Career Services Department for information and resources.

Visit websites to find salary information related to your industry.

Talk to professors, friends, and relatives within your industry.

Figure out what salary you can afford to live on and what other benefits you will need.

Set realistic salary expectations based on industry standards. Don't over or undersell yourself.

Never be the first to bring up salary. Let the employer/ recruiter take the lead.

If offered a salary that does not fall within your range, you can come back with one offer. Never counteroffer a second time.

Start off with a positive tone– avoid ultimatums and threats. Always consult reputable resources or professionals for advice before attempting to negotiate a salary.

If asked to disclose your salary requirements prior to or during an interview, give a range or state that it is negotiable based upon benefits. Another approach is to carefully turn the question back to them by stating, "I am sure you pay your employees fairly based on the industry standard. I would be interested to learn what your salary range might be for this position."

Never underestimate the value of a good benefit package. Before negotiating the bottom line, ask about health insurance benefits and cost, sick time, holiday/ vacation time, 401(k)/ 403 (b), tuition reimbursement, etc. to fully understand your package. Your benefit package will be worth thousands. You may want to consider less salary for outstanding benefits.

Websites to use for salary guides or information:

    www.hotjobs.com
    www.monster.com
    www.salary.com
    www.careerbuilder.com

NOTES

SENIOR COURSE

Week # 5 - 7: Senior Choice Programs

In place of regular class meetings for the month of October, seniors must attend 4 of about 20 programs offered. Most programs are led by business professionals, corporate recruiters, and/or alumni. Topics include: Negotiating Salary & Benefits, First Year on the Job, Resumes/Cover Letters In-depth, Mock Interview with a Recruiter, Women in Business, Using the Internet for a Job Search, Networking, Etiquette Dinner, Experience-Sharing with a Freshman Seminar Class, Career Options for Liberal Arts Majors, Renting an Apartment/Buying a Car, Advanced Interviewing Skills, Staying Fit for Life, Post-graduation Options, Effectively Using the Portfolio in an Interview, and more

NOTES

SENIOR CHOICE PROGRAMS

This form must be completed to receive credit for attending

Name(print): _____ Signature_____

PDS Instructor Name:_____ Day/Time of Class: _____

Title of Program: _____Today's Date:_____

	No/Not very				Yes/Very
The program topic is important to me	1	2	3	4	5
The program content was informative	1	2	3	4	5
The program materials used were helpful	1	2	3	4	5
The speaker was knowledgeable about the topic	1	2	3	4	5
The day/time/location were good	1	2	3	4	5
Overall, the presentation was valuable	1	2	3	4	5

Comments:

SENIOR COURSE

Week # 8: Self Assessment

Your faculty member will distribute various assessments for you to take. It has been found that the better we understand ourselves and our achievements and skills, the better we can communicate these to others. This is especially important in the interview process. Therefore, these self assessments will aid you in your job search and beyond.

NOTES

SENIOR COURSE

Week # 9: Ethics and Professionalism/ Networking

NOTES

ETHICS AND PROFESSIONALISM

CASE STUDY #1

Peter is a senior Accounting major at Nichols College. He completed his internship at a local CPA firm in the fall of his senior year. The internship went well and in December, just before his internship was completed, his supervisor offered him a full-time position beginning in May. Peter asked if he could think about it for a few days. He did, and since he had no other options at the time, he accepted a few days later.

In January Peter began to wonder if this position was really what he wanted so he began a job search. In February he was offered another position, one which he was sure he would like. He accepted this position and called the first company to decline. The first company was not pleased as they had already printed his business cards and the name sign for his door. They had also lost valuable recruiting time to hire someone else.

Was Peter right in doing what he did? Why or why not?

CASE STUDY # 2:

This is an actual letter received from a graduate of the Class of 2005, sent to the Director of Career Services in the summer of 2005. The name of the recent graduate and the company/department has been changed.

"This is Tonya Jones, a recent college graduate. I am having difficulties with making or thinking of making some decisions about jobs. I need your advice. You were the first person I thought of that could possibly help give some guidance. I am currently working at ABC Company in the IT department as a Data Assistant to the Business Operations/IT Manager. The job pays by salary in the lower twenty thousands. This position is not as challenging as I thought it would be but I made the decision to accept the job because it is a full-time job with benefits. I have been here working at ABC Company for about three weeks now, and recently I've found other job [opportunities] in my area, the salary is higher in the thirty thousands and requires more responsibilities and a degree where as ABC did not. What do I do? I'm not sure if I should stick it out with ABC for 6 months or more, or apply at these other places and be more challenged? I don't want to make any un-professional decisions that can make me look bad, I need your advice."

What should Tonya do? Why?

CASE STUDY # 3:

Tom Davidson is a senior who has his heart set on working for Applewood Corporation as a salesperson. He knows several people who work there and others who have in the past. He knows he can be very successful in this position and longs to be part of this growing, dynamic company. Tom has learned from researching the company that their minimum GPA for salespeople is 3.0. Tom's GPA is 2.78. Should he put on his resume that he has a 3.0 GPA? He feels confident about presenting himself well in an interview, but he needs to obtain the interview. He knows his slightly lower GPA may be the factor that prevents him from getting the interview. He wants desperately to pass the resume screening and "shine" in an interview.

Should Tom put a 3.0 on his resume? What should he put on an application? Is it wrong to list his GPA as 3.0?

CASE STUDY # 4:

Susan Thompson is a motivated senior who has been busy in the search for a full-time position after graduation. She has interviewed with 5 companies. One company, On Time Industries, offered her a position with a salary of $28,000. She likes the position and company, but asks the company for some time to think about the offer. She would really like to make $32,000, and hopes that a higher offer may be made from another company that she is even more interested in, Blue Sky Enterprises. Blue Sky calls her and offers her a position paying $30,000. Susan decides that she will try to negotiate a salary at Blue Sky for $32,000. She tells Blue Sky that she has another offer for $32,000 (which she does not) and she is wondering if Blue Sky will match that offer. They ask which company offered her $32,000.

Should Susan have told Blue Sky that she had a higher offer than she really had? What does she tell the recruiter when they ask which company offered her that much?

NETWORKING FOR SUCCESS
Steps for Successful Networking

What is Networking?
"Networking is the on-going process of creating connections and nurturing relationships that benefit both parties over time." (Nierenberg, n.d.)
Networking is an attitude, an approach to life. In a network, the secret is to give power away. Networking is a spirit of giving and sharing.

Why Network?
- A referral generates 80 percent more results than a cold call.
- Approximately 70 percent of all jobs are found through networking.
- Most people you meet have at least 250 contacts.
- Anyone you might want to meet or contact is only four to five people away from you.
  A network will:
- Replace the weakness of the individual with the strength of the group. However, networking is not a team sport - it is an individual sport, created with the help of others.
- Be a support system for honest feedback.
- Will keep one's enemies/competitors close for observation. As the saying goes, "Keep your friends close and your enemies even closer."
- Allow you to help others while helping yourself.

Who Should Be In Your Network?
- Not your immediate family, but their contacts should be.
- People who: are honest, have connections, have a solid reputation, you can offer help to, will help you when needed.
- Older, more experienced people - they may have more time to give to you, have the wealth of experience, enjoy being asked their opinion.
- "Best bet: family advisor, particularly a lawyer or banker, a rich relative, one of your parents' bosses at work, anyone old, experienced in business, with a wide range of contacts and some personal or professional connection to your family." (Mackay)
- People you meet personally at social events
- People you meet professionally at conventions, conferences, professional organizations, meetings.

Build a Network
- Build a network now, before you need it.
- Where to start: 1) College Alumni Clubs 2) Industry Associations 3) Social Clubs (Rotary, Lions Club, golf courses/country clubs, etc.) 4) Hobbies (people in middle age have more time and money for a renewed interest in their hobbies and bring a wealth of experience and advice to give).
- It's not what you know, but who you know, and more importantly: who knows you.
- Create a list of your possible contacts.
- Recognize and appreciate the people in your network. Send handwritten thank you notes, birthday cards, holiday cards. Don't forget their children, their graduations, accomplishments.
- Create a diverse network: age, background, ethnicity, gender, etc.
- Safeguard and nurture your network.
- Be committed to the success of the people in your network.

How to Network

- Go, join, participate. Get out and meet people, make opportunities for yourself. Always be open to meeting others, consider everyone to be of importance.
- Meet everyone you can. Talk to people, even people you may not have previously spoken with. Three foot rule.
- Generate conversation, ask open-ended questions, reintroduce yourself rather than wait for them to remember you. Build rapport before sharing business cards.
- Business cards - write short comment on back: where met, impression, facts, other contacts, date.
- Put yourself in the way of people with influence: fly first class if possible, save up for a membership at an exclusive golf club, etc. Not so you can impress, but who can impress you?
- Be an active participant in any interaction: listen, pay attention to facial and body expressions, remember the person's name, focus on the person so you will remember their face and interesting facts, smile, be positive, show your manners.
- Ask what you can do for them. And do it, as long as it is possible, ethical and moral. Give to their charity, volunteer at their fund-raiser, etc. Your time is the easiest way to give.
- Ask for advice, not for a job.
- Once you ask for their advice, and they give it, they are invested in you and your future. Your failure or success will be a reflection on them and the strength of their own network.
- Tell people what you are looking for: do they know anyone who may understand the value of adding someone with experience in a given field to a particular type of industry?
- Do your homework before meeting someone important: their latest accomplishments, their birthday, hobbies/interests, etc. Use newsletters, internet, library, your network.
- Read. Be informed of current events, new ideas in the industry, up and coming people, etc.
- Know the gatekeeper- this person has importance since they were hired and are trusted by whom you are trying to reach, learn his/her name, make small talk, treat him/her with respect, say "I would like to work directly with you".
- Remember, networking is a learned behavior, and failure will come more frequently in the beginning. Stay confident and focused: you will succeed!

NETWORKING FOR SUCCESS

Who Inspires You?

Each month create a list of people who inspire you. You could add one name a day, or add several names once a month. The list may include a speaker, an author, a colleague, a key person in your organization or at organization you might want to belong to someday, or someone in your field who has recently accomplished something. In order to network effectively, you need to reach out to others, particularly to people of influence. Be realistic about who you try to develop a networking relationship with. You will want to include people with whom you have a real chance of developing a networking relationship.

After creating your list of names and including the date, send these people a note. The note may be a congratulatory one, a note of introduction, or one asking a question or asking their opinion. However, be sure that this opportunity to connect is not all about you. Keep the focus on the other person and their accomplishments.

Month: _____

Name/Reason	Date Added	Note Sent
1.		
2.		
3.		
4.		
5.		
6.		
7.		
8.		
9.		
10.		
11.		
12.		
13.		
14.		
15.		
16.		
17.		
18.		
19.		
20.		
21.		
22.		
23.		
24.		
25.		
26.		
27.		
28.		
29.		
30.		
31.		

Comments/Notes:

NOTES

SENIOR COURSE

Weeks # 10-11: Presentations- Senior Project

NOTES

SENIOR PROJECT GRADING RUBRIC

Group Member Names: _____

_____

Date of Presentation: _____

TOPIC	VALUE – POINTS	POINTS EARNED	COMMENTS
Introduction – group members, state topic and its value in the job search	5		
Comprehensive presentation, including major highlights	30		
Strengths/weaknesses of using this in a search	10		
Why this should be part of a job search	10		
Engagement of students – use of media, activity, or classroom discussion	10		
Summary, wrap-up	5		
One page summary of highlights/ recommendations	20		
Group membership – equality of work and presentation	10		
TOTAL	100		

NOTES

PRESENTATION PEER EVALUATION SHEET

Presenter's Name: _____

Evaluator's Name: _____

I.   <u>CONTENT</u>

    A. Quality and quantity of information

        Poor   1   2   3   4   5   Excellent

    B. Analysis of data, interpretation, discussion questions, explanation

        Poor   1   2   3   4   5   Excellent

II.   <u>PRESENTATION</u>

    A. Organization, smooth transition between ideas, clear introduction and summary

        Poor   1   2   3   4   5   Excellent

    B. Clearly spoken/articulated, not too fast or too slow, volume, delivery

        Poor   1   2   3   4   5   Excellent

III.   <u>COMMENTS</u>

NOTES

SENIOR COURSE

Week # 12: Affective & Transition Issues/
First Year on the Job

NOTES

LEAVING COLLEGE

Make a timeline that starts 2 years before you started college and ends 5 years from now. Mark as many personal, social, academic and career landmarks as you can think of on the line.

Then answer each of the following questions:

What are you most looking forward to leaving behind from college?

What will be the hardest thing to leave?

What has been the most difficult aspect of the last 3 1/2 years?

What has been the best aspect?

What has been the most significant change in YOU between the time you were in high school and the time you have been in college?

What would you like to change in yourself in the next 5 years?

NOTES

FIRST YEAR ON THE JOB

Compare how your life is senior year with how you expect it to be when you are working
at your first professional job. Who determines these factors in your life now? Who will determine
them when you are working?

	College Years	New Job/ Professional Life
Dress		
Sleep Pattern		
People You Spend Time With		
Who's in Charge		
Speech/Language		
Work Time Vs. Play Time		
Feedback on Your Performance		
Other		

FIRST YEAR ON THE JOB

Compare how your life is senior year with how you expect it to be when you are working
at your first professional job. Who determines these factors in your life now? Who will determine
them when you are working?

	College Years	New Job/ Professional Life
Dress		
Sleep Pattern		
People You Spend Time With		
Who's in Charge		
Speech/Language		
Work Time Vs. Play Time		
Feedback on Your Performance		
Other		

FIRST YEAR ON THE JOB

1) TIME FRAME

First Day
Make a good overall first impression
Arrive early
Dress for success
Communicate well- active listener, speak confidently, firm hand shake, eye
    contact, warm smile, ask questions
Remember a few names, write down the most important ones, ask if you don't
    remember
People may ignore you or people may go out of their way to acknowledge you
Some nervousness, anxiety is ok, but try to relax
Be humble
Be nice first
Show a sincere desire to join the group
Be positive!
Observe the environment
Seek clarification if confused
Be a sponge and absorb all you can

First Week
Build rapport – assist others, ask for assistance, learn from a variety of people
Listen – to instructions, don't interrupt, write things down, pay attention
Be positive – enthusiastic, confident, courteous
Watch your environment – much of your learning will be experiential
Production- strive for quality, quantity will come, too much to do – prioritize, too
    little to do – job shadow
Meet with supervisor at end of week for clarification on job duties
Do grunt work!
Take the initiative, even when the unexpected happens
Observe the larger world that you are now part of – administration, other
    departments, etc.
Own up to mistakes – they are yours, people are watching
Learn the most important tasks/responsibilities first
Complete lots of forms – Human Resources, departmental
Set up voice mail, learn official form of communication in company, etc.

First Month

Determine supervisor's expectations – repeat them back to him/her
Listen and learn
Use time wisely
Show eagerness to learn, be productive
Be a team player – no gossiping or speaking negatively of others
Be a self-starter
Begin search for a mentor
Observe the company culture in action
Learn who's really in charge and who's there to help you
Age can mean wisdom – watch and learn
Follow through with commitments
Develop new relationships
Learn to "smooze" – for a few minutes, build rapport
Set goals for personal achievement
Don't appear like you have all of the answers
Never criticize procedures
Get to know 6 new people
Ask supervisor how you are doing and be open to hear the answer

Month Two and Beyond

Get something done – demonstrate your value
Write your job description and compare with the one you were given
Keep the energy, enthusiasm going
Volunteer for company events/programs – you will be giving to the company in
          another way, it will be recognized by important people, and you will meet
          new people!
Continue to be open to learn, learn, learn

2) GETTING ALONG WITH OTHERS

Getting Along with the Supervisor

Accept criticism, be open and learn from it, it is given so you can be successful
Be loyal, help the boss look good
Admit your mistakes
Ask for feedback
Speak directly with your boss first regarding problems
Bring forth suggestions/solutions
Be humble, not defensive
Don't present bad news early in the day or early in the week
Respect their time – use it wisely
Always be positive about others, including the boss
Don't upstage the boss
Share your successes humbly

Getting Along with Co-workers

Learn to work with people you don't like
Be a team player
Control your emotions, your opinions and your temper
Respect differences
Deal directly with co-workers to resolve issues
Listen to others
Show respect – use manners
Be cooperative – don't blame others, you are all part of the same team
Use common sense
If unresolved problems exist, seek help from boss
Be happy, smile!

Getting Along with Customers and Other Professionals

Treat them the way you want to be treated
Meet their needs the best you can
Listen closely, speak clearly
Your company's reputation is based on what the customer thinks of YOU!
Build a solid network with others, it will help make your job easier, and fun

3) TIPS FOR SUCCESS

Manage your time wisely
Learn to de-stress
Stay positive
Be part of the solution, not part of the problem
Work hard – arrive early, work late
Ask others what you can do to help
Volunteer
Work toward promotions
Remain marketable

SENIOR COURSE

Course Evaluation

NOTES

SENIOR PDS COURSE EVALUATION

Name *(OPTIONAL)* _____ Section #_____ Semester _____

In order to provide the best Professional Development Seminar program possible, we need your opinion of this course. All answers are confidential and only averages will be presented. Please provide your honest opinions.

► **DEMOGRAPHIC INFORMATION:**

1. Sex: □   Male   Female   □   **2. College Major:** _____

3. Year in College: 1st □   2nd □   3rd □   4th □   other □

► **YOUR OPINIONS OF THIS COURSE:**

1. In your opinion, what was the **best** thing or the most valuable experience about this course?

2. The **worst**?

3. Would you be willing to return next year and describe this course to next year's class?
Yes   No

4. If you were to return to next year's class, what advice would you offer those students?

► **YOUR OPINION OF THE CONTENT OF THIS COURSE:**

INSTRUCTIONS: please check the box on the right that corresponds to your opinion of each question below from *strongly disagree, disagree, no opinion, agree* and *strongly agree.*

♦ *This course helped me to...*	SD	D	N	A	SA
1. Gain a better understanding of my **personal** goals; how college can help achieve them					
2. Gain a better understanding of my **career** goals; how college can help achieve them					
2. Understand how I am responsible for my college experience and making plans to guarantee my college success.					

► **SELF EVALUATION:**

The amount of work I did for this course was...

|---------------+--------------+--------------+--------------+--------------+------------|
Quite a lot   Average   Very little

I am now aware that the time I spent was...

|---------------+--------------+--------------+--------------+--------------|
More than enough   Just right   Not nearly enough

The quality of my work for this course was...

|---------------+--------------+--------------+--------------+--------------|
Excellent   Average   Poor

I learned...

|---------------+--------------+--------------+--------------+--------------|
Very Much   Average   Very little

► **YOUR EVALUATION OF DIFFERENT PARTS OF THIS COURSE:**

INSTRUCTIONS: Please express your opinion of each question by placing a mark between each word. Please read each set of words carefully.
For example:

♦ *The course syllabus was...*

Clear...	____|____|__x_|____|____|____|____	Vague
Casual...	____|____|____|____|____|_x_|____	Professional
Superficial...	____|____|__x_|____|____|____|____	Complete

♦ *My General opinion of the course is...*

Valuable	____|____|____|____|____|____|____	Useless
Challenging	____|____|____|____|____|____|____	Easy
Frustrating	____|____|____|____|____|____|____	Enjoyable
Boring	____|____|____|____|____|____|____	Interesting

♦ *In my opinion, the course assignments are...*

Valuable	____|____|____|____|____|____|____	Useless
Challenging	____|____|____|____|____|____|____	Easy
Frustrating	____|____|____|____|____|____|____	Enjoyable
Boring	____|____|____|____|____|____|____	Interesting

♦ *In my opinion, the time spent in class was...*

Valuable	____|____|____|____|____|____|____	Useless
Challenging	____|____|____|____|____|____|____	Easy
Frustrating	____|____|____|____|____|____|____	Enjoyable
Boring	____|____|____|____|____|____|____	Interesting

► **YOUR EVALUATION OF THE INDIVIDUAL COURSE TOPICS/ASSIGNMENTS:**
How <u>valuable</u> or <u>important</u> do you feel each topic covered this semester is?

INSTRUCTIONS: Please rate each of the following topics from **1 = "not valuable/important"** to **3 = "no opinion or neutral"** to **5 = "very valuable/important"** by marking the corresponding box to the right of each topic

♦ *I would rate the value of the following topics as...*	1	2	3	4	5
	not		avg		very
a) Introduction – Portfolio review, introduction to course...............					
b) Recruiting Options...					
c) How to Use the Portfolio in an Interview..................................					
d) Finances/Budgeting..					
e) Senior Choice Programs – overall..					
f) Myers-Briggs/Self Assessments..					
g) Business Ethics/Etiquette..					
h) Transition from Nichols to Work/Grad School.........................					
i) Senior PDS Group Project..					
j) Individual Recruiting Plan..					
k) Portfolio Development/Process..					
l) Senior PDS Overall..					

SENIOR PDS FACULTY/INSTRUCTOR EVALUATION

Faculty/Instructor Name:_____

Section #_____ Semester _____

EVALUATION OF THE FACULTY/INSTRUCTOR:

The Course Faculty/Instructor…

	Strongly Disagree	Disagree	Neutral/ No opinion	Agree	Strongly agree
1. Was prepared and organized	☐	☐	☐	☐	☐
2. Was knowledgeable	☐	☐	☐	☐	☐
3. Expressed ideas clearly	☐	☐	☐	☐	☐
4. Encouraged class participation	☐	☐	☐	☐	☐
5. Demonstrated respect for the students	☐	☐	☐	☐	☐
6. Was enthusiastic	☐	☐	☐	☐	☐
7. Answered questions clearly & logically	☐	☐	☐	☐	☐
8. Used class time appropriately	☐	☐	☐	☐	☐
9. Was available outside of class	☐	☐	☐	☐	☐

Comments: